IDENTITY!

A SPIRITUAL SELF-MASTERY GUIDE

Is a Call to Return Home

You are not here to become someone else. You are here to remember and embrace the unique, powerful, radiant self that you are. It's a journey of ***returning home*** to your most authentic self, beyond fear, the false self, limitation, and expectations. Spiritual self-mastery is about aligning your inner truth to create your outer reality — living with clarity, courage, and conviction.

Sopheia McMorris

COPYRIGHT

Copyright © 2025 by Sopheia McMorris
All rights reserved.
No part of this book may be copied, distributed, or transferred in any form or by any means without the written permission of the owner, except in the case of brief quotations and critical reviews.
Scripture quotations, where used, are taken from translations of the Holy Bible.
The material in this book has been written and published solely for educational purposes. The author and the publisher shall not be responsible or liable to any person or entity for any loss, damages, or disservice caused or claims caused directly or indirectly by the information included in this book.
These are the statements and opinions of the author and do not reflect the views of the publisher or indicate an endorsement.
Request permission, or write to the publisher at:

Wisdom Speaks Life LLC
sopheia@sopheiaspeakswisdom.com
 https://sopheiaspeakswisdom.com/

Printed in the United States of America.
ISBN: 979-8-9933528-1-7

BONUS!

*IDENTITY! A SPIRITUAL SELF-MASTERY GUIDE:
affirmations, quotes, and mentoring. Learn how to
become who you are and live from your true IDENTITY.
As a bonus, you will receive 20 Powerful Identity
affirmations, 20 Powerful Identity quotes, and mentoring
designed to help you remember and embrace your truth,
identity, freedom, and power to create a life you love.*

Go here: calendly.com/sopheiaspeakswisdom

I look forward to meeting you!

CONTENTS

BONUS

Acknowledgments

Cover Story

Introduction

Chapter One: Awareness and Presence

Awakening, Awareness "Who am I?"

The Masks We Wear and Why They Limit Us

Practicing Presence is A Daily Spiritual Exercise

Wisdom Spiritual Insight

Wisdom Spiritual Declaration

NOTES

Chapter Two: Detachment from False Pride

Freedom from the False Self

Know Yourself Deeply

The False Self/Ego

Wisdom Spiritual Insight

Wisdom Spiritual Declaration

You are Transforming from IDENTITY to BELIEF

NOTES

Chapter Three: Inner Peace a Natural State

Returning to Peace Within

Peace is Not Passive. It's Power.

Cultivate Peace Daily

Wisdom Spiritual Insight

Wisdom Spiritual Declaration

Chapter Four: Alignment with Higher Self and Purpose

Remembering Who You Are and Why You're Here

Align Your Vision and Values

Living from Your Higher Self

Wisdom Spiritual Insight

Wisdom Spiritual Declaration

Transformation from BELIEVE to BECOME

NOTES

Chapter Five: Accepting Your Shadow

Bring Light to What's Been Hidden

Heal what Hurts

Walk with Your Shadow in the Light

Wisdom Spiritual Insight

Wisdom Spiritual Declaration

NOTES

Chapter Six: Surrender, Let Go, and Trust

Releasing Control and Resting in Faith

Let Go and Embrace Your Becoming

Love is the Language of Faith

Wisdom Spiritual Insight

Wisdom Spiritual Declaration

NOTES

Chapter Seven: Unity of Oneness

Living from Wholeness

From Separation to Sacred Belonging

Building Discipline and Devotion

Wisdom Spiritual Insight

Wisdom Spiritual Declaration

Transformation From BECOME to BECOMING to BEING

NOTES

8 | Page

Conclusion

A Letter for Embodying Who You
Already Are

Next Steps

About the Author

Endnotes

NOTES

Acknowledgments

With deep gratitude, I honor God my Source, for my wellspring of wisdom, truth, identity, and life, whose presence and guidance breathe through every area of my life and word of this work.

To every person who has participated in my life's journey, especially to those who have allowed me to see God, to see myself and remember my identity, I genuinely thank you! My hope for you is love, joy, and peace, and to always remember your own divine identity.

To God, my father, mentor, teacher, and spiritual guide, who poured wisdom into my journey, whose word, love, light, and divine guidance have helped me remember my true identity. To my sweet loves, who are always here with me, whose lives intertwine with mine, thank you for your love and support, which helped to anchor me in remembrance of who I am.

To seekers, leaders, and readers who would hold this guide in their hands and dare to look within, I wrote this book for you. My intention is to remind you of your divine identity, to inspire you to rise, awaken into your divine becoming, and live as the radiant expression of who you are. May these words affirm your worth and empower you to pursue self-mastery and authenticity.

The truth is that you are already whole, already worthy, already free. Identity is not a destination; it is a lifelong unfolding, a journey of self-discovery and growth. The path of spiritual self-mastery is not about becoming someone else, but about remembering who you already are.

As you begin, I encourage you to approach with an open mind. Come with curiosity. Come ready to let go of what no longer serves you. ***IDENTITY! A SPIRITUAL SELF-MASTERY GUIDE*** is not just a book; it's an invitation to live as your most authentic self, here and now.

Artwork Swan Art 9-2025 by @cataclysm12

Cover Story

I chose a swan because it represents self-discovery, inner beauty, fulfilment, and the triumph of authenticity. It is our true self—the self that waits beneath doubt, rejection, and misunderstanding. It is the beauty you carry even when others cannot see it. It is proof that time and struggle do not destroy you; they reveal who you are.

The swan in The Ugly Duckling is my story, and may be many of your stories. I felt like the duckling wandering around, lost and trying to find home. I felt misunderstood and unloved, judged by my appearances, cast aside, and left to believe I did not belong and could not fit in. But deep within me, I felt the truth of something greater.

As the seasons changed, I grew into who I had always been, seeing my true reflection. I embody transformation, belonging, and authenticity, showing myself that trials and rejection often prepare us to recognize our worth.

The swan represents true, inherent identity and beauty. Your unique qualities that were always present but hidden, forgotten. This transformation symbolizes the realization of your authentic self, personal growth, discovery, reflection, and understanding, which ultimately leads to self-acceptance and a sense of belonging.

When you take the time to remember, you will see that you are more than the names others have given you. You are more than the seasons of loneliness and doubt. You are more than your limitations, more than what you fear you are. Like me, you are becoming what you have always been.

I chose the swan because it is a symbol of identity revealed, potential realized, and embodies the sacred truth that what others see does not define who you are. It shows us that being different is not a failure, but rather a unique expression, and that becoming who we are requires both patience and courage.

Sometimes in life, we find ourselves wandering, unsure, rejected, and feeling forgotten. Oh, but when we look within ourselves and see our true self, radiant and free, that's the moment we awaken to your divine identity.

You will realize that every hardship was sharpening and shaping you into who you already are—revealing the truth of greatness within you.

Introduction

WHO AM I?

For years, humanity has sought the answer to the question of identity. The world, with its momentary achievements, relationships, and roles, cannot define or alter your true self. Your identity, eternal and unchanging, resides within, anchored in Spirit, impervious to the ebb and flow of circumstance.

This guide is a mirror that reminds you of who you already are. Identity is not something you must earn, prove, or perform. It is your birthright, your essence, your divine inheritance.
As you navigate these pages of remembrance, shedding false labels such as 'not good enough', 'unworthy', or 'incomplete'; reclaim your truth and embrace your becoming. Each reflection, each practice, is designed to call you back to yourself, the self beyond fear, beyond doubt, beyond illusion.

Remember, you are not embarking on a journey to become someone new. You are awakening to the truth of who you have always been.

IDENTITY! A SPIRITUAL SELF-MASTERY GUIDE is a trusted companion for your soul, a guiding light along your path. May it help you remember your divine identity, rise into your divine becoming, and live as the radiant expression of who you truly are.

You are here to *remember* your brilliant, authentic, powerful, radiant Self. Within every heart lies a deep longing for peace, purpose, and the power to rise above fear, doubt, and limitation.

IDENTITY! A SPIRITUAL SELF-MASTERY GUIDE is a divine invitation to awaken the truth within you and walk boldly in faith toward your highest Self. It's not a destination but an unfolding of an ongoing process of growth, awareness, and expansion. Self-reflection, resilience, and the willingness to evolve will awaken your highest Self, and you will begin to live not just for survival, but for significance.

IDENTITY is your foundation. Until you know who you truly are, beyond titles, roles, and opinions of others, you will always live as a shadow of yourself. It's time to strip away illusions, reclaim your worth, and start living from it. Know that you are beloved and a creative expression of the Divine.

BELIEF is a transformative bridge. It's the link between who you are now and who you are becoming. Belief takes you from knowing to an unwavering conviction. B*elieve in your divine identity* and let this belief guide your potential.

BECOMING is the embodiment. Discipline, personal development, and mental fortitude are essential to self-mastery; it is also a spiritual journey, the art of surrendering to the Divine within, aligning your life with eternal truth, and living from a place of love, clarity, and inner strength. It involves transcending the shadow, aligning with higher consciousness, and living in harmony with truths. It is living your truth, without deviation from how you present yourself in the world. Allow what you already are to emerge; this is mastery of Self, not control, but alignment.

Self-mastery is not about controlling every part of life. It's about aligning your inner truth, influencing your thinking, feelings, and actions, living with clarity, courage, and conviction. This guide is a journey of *returning home* to your most authentic Self, beyond fear, ego, and expectations. It's about remembering and reconnecting with your most authentic Self. Rooted in purpose, authenticity, and freedom. Empowering you to break free from the external definitions of success and identity, leading to clarity, confidence, and inner peace. It is about becoming whole, living in alignment with your values, and expressing your unique gifts.

Embarking on the journey of Self-discovery and self-actualization is a courageous act. It's about going inward and becoming the highest expression of who you are, thereby fulfilling your potential and realizing your truth. The spiritual aspects of self-mastery center on awakening to the most authentic Self, the essence that exists beyond the mind and illusions. You'll explore the power of belief and the divine potential within you. *IDENTITY!* Challenge you to grow, inspire you to trust, and equip you to overcome, not by might or willpower alone, but with Spirit.

IDENTITY! A SPIRITUAL SELF-MASTERY GUIDE gives you the power to live with clarity, creativity, compassion, and contribution, to become the observer of your thoughts, the student of your emotions, and the architect of your inner and outer world. The answers you seek are within.

This guide is about *remembering*, *reclaiming*, and *revealing*. Through reflection, spiritual principles, and practical steps, you will walk the path from identity to belief to becoming to being. You will find that you are not becoming someone new; you are remembering the fullness of who you are.

Embrace this invitation to rise and become who you are. Let go of limitations and embody your full potential. Embark on a journey of spiritual self-mastery, where your foundation is rooted in identity, belief, and personal growth. Faith is your fuel, and Spirit guides you with truth.

"Do not be conformed to this world but be transformed by the renewing of your mind."

—Romans 12:2

Chapter One

Awareness and Presence

The First Step: Awakening, Awareness "Who am I?"

To start the exciting journey of spiritual self-mastery, you must first welcome the transformative power of acceptance, **awareness**, and awaken to presence. Before one can rise, evolve, or heal, awakening is first and foremost. Awareness acts as the guiding light, illuminating both the inner self and the divine that is present in all existence. Without this awareness, we are mere drifters in life, at the mercy of our emotions, false self, or fear. But with it, we begin to *perceive* the truth.

The journey to mastery does not begin with a battle against your nature, but with a deep understanding and acceptance of it. Before you can truly be who you are, you must first *awaken to your* present state. Presence allows you to feel and observe your emotions and thoughts without being consumed by them. It is the bridge that connects you to your true self. Embracing yourself fully allows you to shed the masks, the roles, labels, and limiting beliefs that have held you back. This act of acceptance is a powerful step towards your spiritual self-mastery, liberating you from the constraints of societal expectations and self-imposed limitations.

Awareness is more than noticing your thoughts or feelings; it is about being **present** in the moment. Presence is where God dwells, where peace is, and where your true power begins. It is in this quiet space within your heart that allows you to reconnect with your Spirit, the part of you that is at peace, wise, and whole. This peace and power are always within your reach, waiting for you to embrace them.

Be Present with Yourself and with the Divine
To master yourself spiritually, you must learn to be present with yourself and with **God**. Spiritual mastery is not a goal; it is a journey that is available in every moment, in the quietness of early morning, in the tension of difficult conversations, in the beauty of sunset, or even in your day-to-day routine. It's a journey that starts with simple, sacred practices and is within your reach, no matter where you are in life.
When you pause and become aware, you shift from a state of survival to *one of spiritual alignment*. You begin to recognize that you are not alone. God is not outside of you in a far-off, distant place. Spirit is within you. When you sit in the present moment, your inner life begins to transform. Anxiety calms, confusion gives way to clarity, and Reaction becomes response. This transformation marks the beginning of your journey to spiritual mastery, a path filled with power, hope, and inspiration.

The Masks We Wear and Why They Limit Us

Before you can remember who, you are, you must first face who you are not. From birth, and throughout the years of your life, layer upon layer of masks and labels attach themselves to your identity. By unmasking these layers, you clear the path to self-discovery.
Mask ties you to the roles you play in life (e.g., parent, partner, professional), making you feel incomplete without them. Although roles are essential, they are not the totality of who you are.

Cultural, societal, or self-imposed labels often dictate our sense of self-worth. Whether it is "success" or "failure," these definitions can confine you. Limiting beliefs, such as "I'm not good enough" or "I don't deserve love," create walls that block your potential.

Identifying too closely with past mistakes, traumas, or achievements makes it challenging to live in the present truth of who you are. By identifying and releasing these masks, you pave the way to reclaiming your divine, authentic self.

Awaken to Your True Identity: Awakening to your true identity is a process of unlearning, rediscovery, and deep connection with your inner essence.

Practicing Self-Inquiry will help you begin this journey with a powerful question: "Who am I?" Reflect on whether you define yourself by your profession, relationships, or past experiences. Explore the origins of your beliefs about yourself and determine whether they hold truth or illusion.

Release Limiting Beliefs about yourself and your identity. Reflect on the beliefs you hold about yourself and your capabilities that feel limiting. Write them down, challenge their validity, and replace them with affirmations that align with your sense of worthiness and potential.

Listen to Your Inner Voice. Your authentic self often speaks through intuition and inner knowing. Commit to a daily prayer, mindfulness, or meditation practice that quiets external noise and allows you to tune into this voice.

Accept Imperfections and know you are Whole. Awakening doesn't mean becoming "perfect" but rather accepting and loving yourself entirely, including your flaws. Practice self-compassion, recognizing that your worth reflects your identity.

Align Your Actions with Your Authentic Self. Living your truth means reevaluating your priorities and focusing your energy on pursuits that align with your truth, such as genuine relationships, purposeful work, and creative passions.

Surround Yourself with Authentic Connections. Take time to think about what you value and seek out relationships that uplift you rather than force you to conform to roles or expectations.

Awakening involves both triumphs and roadblocks. Expect moments of discomfort as you demolish previously held beliefs, labels, and patterns.

Challenges are inevitable; learn how to process and overcome them.

Possible experiences are:

- **Fear of Change:** Remind yourself that letting go of the old makes space for what's more meaningful.
- **Judgment from Others:** Not everyone will understand your awakening. Firmly ground yourself in your inner knowing rather than seeking external approval.
- **Impatience:** Awakening is a lifelong practice. Celebrate every milestone and trust the process.

Practicing Presence is A Daily Spiritual Exercise

You don't have to retreat to a mountain to become spiritually aware. You start with simple, sacred practices:

- **For instance, you can start by breathing deeply and becoming aware of your heart.** Breath is life and a gift from God.
- **Observe without judgment.** Notice your thoughts, emotions, or surroundings. Let them come and go like waves, without attaching a yes or no to them.
- **Acknowledge Spirit's presence.** Whisper, *"I know you are here."* Rest in that truth.

- **Bring your awareness into your day.** Whether cleaning the house, driving, or working, practicing presence means being fully present in the moment, wherever you are. You are not behind in the past. You are not ahead in the future. You are here, here now, in this circumstance or situation where you find yourself. Accept and be present.

Who are you beneath the roles you play, the labels you wear, and the limitations you believe define you? Awareness is the central question driving one of the most significant inner journeys a person can take. But why is this process so necessary, and how can we discover freedom and purpose by peeling away these layers?

Let's examine some of the pitfalls of living disconnected from your identity.

- **Constantly Seeking External Validation:** Building your life on external approval and validation can be exhausting, leading to a perpetual pursuit of accomplishments and affirmation.
- **Making Fear-Based Decisions:** When your identity is rooted in fears, trauma, or limiting beliefs, your actions are dictated by a desire to avoid failure rather than pursuing genuine joy.
- **Loss of Purpose:** Without clarity about who you are at your core, it becomes challenging to connect to a deeper life purpose.
- **Inner Conflict:** Living through masks and roles that feel incongruent with your essence can create doubts, anxiety, and emotional turmoil.

Wisdom Spiritual Insight

When you become present, aware, and accepting, you become an observer of your own life. You are an observer of your thoughts and emotions. *"You see your thought and feel your emotion without forming a conclusion about them.*

Wisdom Awaken to Truth
Remember who you are beyond the roles, labels, and limitations, remember you are whole, worthy, and deeply connected to Spirit.
Awakening to your true self ends the inner struggle. It reveals your inherent sense of worth and your unlimited potential, replacing confusion with clarity and peace. This shift not only transforms your well-being but also inspires authentic connections, creativity, and a more fulfilling life. Your awakening stops the illusions of the false self and reveals a more profound truth: you are not your fears, your failures, traumas, past, or future.

Wisdom Ask Yourself
- What do I believe about myself, and where did that belief come from?
- What parts of me are authentic, and which parts are adapted?

Awaken to yourself, the version untouched by fear, shame, or expectations.

Wisdom Reflection Prompts
- What roles or identities have I taken on that no longer serve me?
- When do I feel most like myself?
- Who was I before the world told me who to be?

Wisdom Exercises
- *Mirror Exercise:* Look into the mirror and speak affirmations of who you are.
- *Inventory your Identity:* Write down labels you've identified with. Cross out any that are not rooted in love or truth.

Your identity is not about performance, appearance, or approval. It is rooted in truth, Spirit, and your true essence. Self-mastery begins by awakening to that truth.

Your Rewards for Living Authentically
The rewards of awakening far outweigh the challenges. Here's what awaits you on the other side of your transformation:
- **Inner Freedom:** Free yourself from the weight of societal expectations and judgments.
- **Deeper Relationships:** A Genuine connection with others will attract like-minded individuals.
- **Purposeful Living:** Experience a sense of alignment and direction as you act in line with your inherent values.
- **Enduring Peace:** Experience quiet confidence, certainty, knowing you are whole without needing validation from outside sources.

Wisdom Reflection Questions
1. When do you feel most present with God?
2. What distracts or triggers you?
3. How can you begin each day with intention, acceptance, and awareness?

Awakening to your true identity is a form of self-love. It requires patience, introspection, perseverance, courage, and a willingness to walk away from what's comfortable, venturing into the unknown.

Wisdom Spiritual Declaration

I surrender and let go of the past and the future. And rest in the present moment. I open my heart to Spirit. Awareness and acceptance are the start of my transformation. I choose love and present awareness.

NOTES

Chapter Two

Detachment from False Pride

The Second Step: Freedom from the False Self

After awakening through awareness, the next step in spiritual self-mastery is **detachment from false pride**, the ego, and the false self. The version of you built by fear, comparison, and pain. It clings to labels, status, control, and image. It says, *"I am what I have, what I do, and what others think of me."* You are none of those things. You are Spirit, a divine essence within you, made in the image of God, the ultimate source of Love and truth. These false layers can be like a mask of pride you wear to hide your insecurities, a performance you put on to please others, or a pretense you maintain to fit in. You *no longer need to prove, perform, or please.* Release the false self and return to truth.

Know Yourself Deeply

To Know Yourself Deeply is the foundation of spiritual self-mastery, for without self-knowledge, you cannot live in alignment with who you are. To know yourself deeply is to look beyond surface roles, labels, and expectations, and to courageously explore the depths of your thoughts, emotions, values, and desires. It requires honesty, reflection, and a willingness to face yourself. Awareness reveals patterns that guide your choices, wounds that need healing, and gifts that you desire to express fully. As you grow in self-knowledge, you discover that the answers you seek outside are within. From that sacred place of clarity, you can live with authenticity, power, and peace.

Self-knowledge is your compass; it involves understanding your values, patterns, emotions, and desires. It guides you towards a purposeful life.

This self-awareness is your tool for empowerment, inspiring you to live with intention and guiding you towards your highest potential.

Tools like journaling, quiet reflection, and mindfulness can help you record your thoughts and feelings, think deeply about yourself, and focus on the present moment.

The False Self/Ego

When we allow our environment, societal expectations, fear, and past conditioning to lead us to separation, comparison, and external validation, we distort our reality and persuade ourselves that we are not enough unless we meet certain standards or possess specific things. Masking our true essence—our inner divinity and authentic self—by promoting fear-based beliefs, defensiveness, and a constant striving to become someone else rather than simply being who we are. The false self keeps us trapped in cycles of suffering, distraction, and disconnection from our inner truth, blocking the path to self-mastery and spiritual liberation.

The false self constantly asks:

- *Am I good enough?*
- *What will others think of me?*
- *How can I stay in control?*

These questions keep you in spiritual bondage. Detachment breaks that cycle. It doesn't mean you don't care. It means you no longer live in fear; now you live in faith. You no longer build your worth on the world's applause. You anchor it in your own and God's approval, knowing that you are already approved. False pride fights for attention;

it's the part of you that seeks validation and approval from others. The Spirit, on the other hand, rests in identity; it's the part of you that is secure in its connection to God and doesn't need external validation. False pride reacts. The Spirit responds. Spiritual self-mastery is choosing truth over the ego's false pride, again and again. Let go and surrender, detachment is an act of **surrender;** it's trusting that God will reveal who you are when you let go of who you *think* you should be.

Wisdom Spiritual Insight

The more you release the false, the more space you create for truth. Detachment is not a loss; it's a return. It's coming back to the still, quiet, unshakable you, held in divine Love. And as the false self fades, peace rises, wisdom sharpens, love deepens, and your spiritual authority strengthens. Detachment is the freedom that we have, the freedom to live from truth. You get to choose what to believe. Let this truth set you free, to have joy, and feel empowered. Detachment is not a loss; it's a liberation.

Wisdom Spiritual Practice
Practice the following to detach from the false self:
- **Notice what triggers you.** When do you feel the need to prove, defend, or control?
- **Pause and breathe**. Step back from reaction.
- **Ask yourself.** What honors truth at this moment?
- **Speak truth.** What does Love say? What does Peace require?

Self-awareness becomes life changing. The deeper and better you understand your thoughts, needs, and triggers, the closer you get to living up to your highest potential.

Wisdom Reflection Prompts

- What emotions do I suppress most often?
- What are my core strengths?
- What patterns keep repeating in my life?

Wisdom Exercises
- *Core Values Discovery:* Use a list of values and circle your top five and define what each means to you.
- *Create an Emotional Awareness Journal:* Track your emotions for seven days. Note what triggered each and how you responded.

Wisdom Reflection Questions
1. Where in your life do you feel controlled by false pride?
2. What identity or role have you clung to that no longer serves your highest good?
3. What surrender practices can you incorporate into your daily routine?

Wisdom Spiritual Declaration

I am letting go of the false; I release the false self's grip on my mind and heart. I lay down fear, pride, and performance. I choose humility over striving, truth over false illusion, and Spirit as the I Am that I Am. Truth is now my guiding light, illuminating my spiritual path.

You are Transforming from IDENTITY to BELIEF!

It's time to trust the truth about who you are. This transition from 'IDENTITY' to 'BELIEF' signifies a deep internalization of your true identity, a belief so strong that it becomes the foundation of your spiritual journey.

NOTES

Chapter Three

Inner Peace as a Natural State

The Third Step: Returning to Peace Within

Now that you have become aware and begun the journey of detachment from the false self, or identity construct based on external factors, you are now ready to embrace one of the most potent benefits of spiritual self-mastery, **Peace. Peace is your natural state.** It is not something you must chase, earn, or achieve; it is who you are when you are aligned. The world teaches us that Peace comes from circumstances, such as paid bills, relationships running smoothly, and goals reached. True Peace is not dependent on anything external. It is the deep stillness of knowing that God's within you, and is for you, no matter who or what surrounds you.

Peace Is Not Passive. It's Power!

It's the inner strength that allows you to face life's uncertainties with a clear mind and a tender heart. Peace is power and certainty within, a quiet force of truth that fuels resilience.

When you walk in Peace

- Your mind becomes clear, even when life is uncertain.
- Your heart stays soft, even when you experience hardship.
- Your spirit grounds you, even when the world shakes.

Peace does not mean you feel nothing; it means *that nothing rules you* except truth. It is a quiet strength, a still assurance that allows you to remain anchored, whole and complete. This kind of Peace comes from knowing the truth. It flows from surrender.

What are the Obstacles that cause you to lose touch with your Inner Peace?
- **Fear distracts you.**
- **Having false pride stirs chaos.**
- **The past is pulling you backward.**
- **The future is filling you with anxiety.**

The invitation of spiritual self-mastery is a call to *return.* Return to the center. Return to trust. Return to truth. When you believe that Peace is already within you, you stop looking outward and start turning inward. You start quieting the noise and *be still and know with certainty.*

Cultivate Peace Daily

To access and protect your inner Peace, do these practices.
- **Begin your day in stillness.** Before screens or schedules, sit and be still. Breathe. Invite Peace.
- **Guard your inner space.** Not everything deserves your energy. Say no to what disturbs your Peace.
- **Choose to respond and not react.** It doesn't mean to ignore reality; instead, you face it with calm authority.
- **Declare Peace aloud.** When you feel life's chaotic, speak calmly to it and reflect on what brings you certainty.

Challenge Limiting Beliefs that disrupt Peace.

What you believe shapes how you behave. Often, hidden beliefs are the roadblocks to becoming who you truly are.

Challenge limiting thoughts like:
- I'm not good enough.

- I have to be perfect.
- I'll never change.

Replace limiting beliefs with truths:

- I am worthy.
- I am making progress.
- I choose to change.

Create freedom within, and you will create freedom in your life. Your beliefs can either expand you or confine you.

Wisdom Spiritual Insight

You were born to live from a place of divine calm. Peace is your divine inheritance. Spiritual self-mastery is a quiet, inward journey, gentle and deeply rooted, and at its center is Peace.

Wisdom Reflection Prompts

- What belief is holding you back right now?
- Where did that belief come from?
- What would you do if you believed you were unstoppable?

Wisdom Exercises

- **Belief Reframe:** Identify one limiting belief and write three empowering thoughts you can believe.
- **Gather Information:** Write about an early memory where you first felt "not enough." What would your higher self say to that version of you?

Wisdom Reflection Questions

1. When do you feel most at Peace within yourself?
2. What steals your Peace, and how can you protect it more intentionally?
3. How would your life change if you lived from a place of Peace?

Wisdom Spiritual Declaration

Today, I return to Peace within me. I release fear, worry, and stress. I receive Peace that calms every storm in my heart. I live in and from Peace. It is who I am.

NOTES

Chapter Four

Alignment with Higher Self and Purpose

The Fourth Step: Alignment Remembering Who You Are and Why You're Here

Once you've awakened to awareness, loosened the grip of the false self, and reconnected with peace within, you are ready to take the next sacred step on the path of spiritual self-mastery: **alignment.**

Align Your Vision and Values

Writing out your vision and values is a way to live with purpose. Your vision provides a clear picture of the life you desire to create, while your values support you as your foundation. When your values and vision align, they become your internal compass, reflecting your highest truth.

Who are you becoming? Define your *why*, your mission, and your guiding principles.

Ask yourself:
- What do I stand for?
- What impact do I want to make?
- What kind of energy do I want to embody?

Let your values lead. Let your vision pull you forward like a lighthouse in the fog, guiding you to safety.

Without healing the pain and trauma, they will keep you from fully embracing your true self. Healing is an act of courage and love; it is the light that shines in dark places.

When your vision and values are clear, your life becomes purposeful, causing you to live by design.

Align your Higher Self with your divine purpose.
Your Higher Self is not a future version of you; it is your *eternal Spirit* that already exists. It is the part of you that remembers truth even when life gets messy. The more you align with your spiritual self, the more you live out your divine calling. Alignment empowers you with clarity, courage, and confidence. Discover your purpose and embrace it; *that is* spiritual alignment. Your purpose invites you to become who you are.

Living from Your Higher Self

Your Higher Self is your Spirit, pure, connected to God, and full of divine wisdom. When you live from that space:

- You choose to respond to life from love, not fear.
- You choose purpose over pressure.
- You follow your inner conviction, not outer comparison.
- You trust that you are divinely supported and divinely guided, even when the path's not visible.

Alignment with your Higher Self means letting go of who you or others *think* you should be and listening deeply to the voice of truth. It is choosing faith over doubt. It allows your inner peace to lead, rather than your outer performance.

Things that Disrupt Alignment?
- **Busyness without intention.**
- **People-pleasing and self-abandonment.**
- **Living by default rather than by design.**
- **Forgetting your true identity.**

When you drift from or start to forget your true identity, you may feel anxious, overwhelmed, or out of sync with yourself. Realign in stillness, prayer, and belief to lead you back to truth.

Wisdom Spiritual Insight

You have a divine calling that only *you* can fulfill. Aligning with the truth leads you to begin transforming, which has a lasting impact.

Your desires, dreams, and convictions are tools for transformation. You don't have to push, fight, or struggle; embrace the fact that you are enough. *Only believe truth.*

Wisdom Spiritual Practice
Daily Align with Your Higher Self and Purpose
- **Pause each day to reconnect.** Ask yourself: *"Am I acting from my spirit, or my ego?"*
- **Journal with Spirit.** Write out: *Who am I today? What is my next faithful step?*
- **Speak life over your identity.** Declare: *"I am aligned. I am loved."*
- **Take aligned, inspired action.** Small steps in truth lead to divine purpose.

Wisdom Reflection Prompts
- What kind of person am I becoming?
- What legacy do I want to leave?
- What values are non-negotiable in my life?

Wisdom Exercises
- **Create a Vision Board:** Create a visual or digital collage representing who you're becoming.
- **Honor Yourself Letter:** Write a letter from yourself, 5 years ahead, wise, peaceful, and aligned.

Wisdom Reflection Questions
1. What does my Higher Self know that fear stops me from remembering?

2. What area of my life feels misaligned with who God created me to be?
3. What is one step I can take to move into a deeper alignment with my purpose?

Wisdom Spiritual Declaration

Now, I release fear, doubt, and distraction. I remember who I am, the version of me that's established in truth and guided by peace. I embrace truth, trusting that God will reveal my purpose to me. I am connected, faithful, and fully present. I am chosen and capable.

You are Transforming from BELIEVE to BECOME!

What you believe shapes every step you take; let your life mirror your truth.

NOTES

Chapter Five

Accepting Your Shadow

The Fifth Step: Bringing Light to What's Been Hidden

Spiritual self-mastery is not about becoming perfect; it is about becoming whole. **Accept your Shadow.** Wholeness requires that we turn toward the parts of ourselves we've tried to hide, silence, or ignore. This step is an honest, humbling, and healing process of acknowledging the darker aspects of oneself, not to judge them, but to **transform** them. Your 'shadow' is not your enemy. It is the collection of hidden fears, wounds, traumas, behaviors, and beliefs that you've disowned or buried to survive or be accepted. In simpler terms, your shadow is the part of you that you've hidden away because it's painful or embarrassing. In psychological terms, the shadow is a concept introduced by Swiss psychiatrist Carl Jung, representing the unconscious aspects of the personality. It holds the parts of you that were silenced by shame or shaped by trauma. What remains hidden will always control you. Spiritual maturity calls you to **bring your shadow, that inner child that is still present within you, into the Light**, where healing becomes possible and love becomes unconditional.

Why Embrace the Shadow?
Because avoiding it keeps you bound and wounded.
Because denying it keeps you divided and separated from your true identity.
Because fearing it keeps you small, afraid to become who you are.

The shadow isn't a sign of weakness; it is awareness of it as a **sacred invitation** to begin your transformation. When you face your darkness with grace, you exhibit immense courage, turning fear into strength, shame into compassion, and limitation into **liberation. You stop running from yourself and start loving yourself fully and truthfully.**

Heal What Hurts

Healing What Hurts is the invitation to bring tenderness to the places within your heart that carry pain, fear, or unspoken wounds. Healing does not mean erasing the past or pretending the hurt never happened; it means allowing love, truth, and compassion to flow into your heart space. When you choose to face your pain with courage instead of avoidance, you open the door for transformation. The process is sacred; what once felt like a weight becomes wisdom. Healing your hurts is not a sign of weakness but a profound act of self-mastery, for it allows your heart to heal, your soul to rise, and your spirit to shine more fully in its divine light.

Healing your hurts requires courage and compassion, especially when you avoid facing the wounds you have buried, denied, or run from. This pain that goes unhealed can become the silent architect of our thoughts, choices, and relationships. When you look into your heart with honesty and grace, and begin to unravel the stories you've carried, releasing the emotional weight you've held on to. You start healing your wounds and chasing off your fears. Your trauma becomes a steppingstone to reclaiming your power. Through self-awareness, forgiveness, and love, you transform your pain into wisdom, your scars into strength, and your past into profound understanding and wholeness.

You pave the way for transformation, bringing hope and optimism that light the way to your future.

To become whole, you must face what has separated you from truth. Spiritual self-mastery, involves integrating all aspects of yourself, is a key part of this process. It's about understanding and accepting all parts of your being, including the painful ones, and using that understanding to guide your actions and thoughts.

Give yourself space to grieve, release, heal, and forgive yourself and others.
- Heal childhood wounds
- Confront betrayal and abandonment
- Let go of resentment and regret

Healing is the deepest act of strength. What you heal within changes the way you see everything. Healing helps you to embrace your true self fully.

Healing what hurts is both an inner and outer journey. It's important to

Acknowledge your Pain – Healing begins with honesty. Allow yourself to name what hurts without judgment or denial. Suppressed pain only deepens over time.

Create Space for Stillness – Slow down enough to listen to your inner voice. Journaling, prayer, or meditation can help you connect with the more profound truth beneath the pain.

Feel and Heal – Give yourself permission to feel the emotions fully—whether grief, anger, sadness, or fear. Emotions lose their grip when they are expressed and released in healthy ways.

Seek Understanding, Not Blame – Instead of asking "Why me?", shift to "What is this teaching me?" Pain often carries hidden wisdom that points toward growth, boundaries, or freedom.

Invite Compassion – Speak to yourself as you would to a dear friend. Replace self-criticism with gentleness. Forgiveness is a gift you give to yourself and others; it is the doorway to peace.

Choose Support – A trusted friend, mentor, or spiritual guide can hold space for your process and remind you that you're not alone. Their presence can provide comfort and strength, making the journey less intimidating.

As the hurt softens, weave the lessons into your daily life. Healing helps you become stronger, wiser, and more whole. When you apply the realization, insights, and wisdom you've gained from your healing into your daily decisions and actions, you create a more fulfilling and authentic life. Healing what hurts is an unfolding of patience, presence, and love.

Walk with Your Shadow in the Light

Walking with Your Shadow in the Light is a bold and empowering act. It is about embracing every part of yourself—both the brilliance and the brokenness—with compassion and truth. Your shadow is not your enemy; it is a teacher that reveals where healing, forgiveness, and integration are needed. Bringing your shadow into the Light of awareness, you no longer shrink or hide in shame; you allow it to guide you toward wholeness. The walk you take now is not about erasing your darkness; it's about letting the Light of your Divine essence illuminate it, transforming wounds into wisdom and pain into power. In walking with your shadow in the Light, you discover that your identity is not defined by what you fear or repress, but by the radiance that shines through when all parts of you are aligned.

Shadow Work Looks Like

- **Facing your inner critic.** The voice that says you're not enough is often a wound disguised as truth.
- **Recognizing unhealthy patterns.** Repeating cycles, continuing to go around the mountain, often point to unhealed places.
- **Exploring your triggers.** Emotional reactions reveal where pain still abides.
- **Acknowledge your fears.** What you refuse to acknowledge will continue to control you.
- **Allowing emotion without judgment.** Tears, anger, and grief are all opportunities to heal.

Shadow work takes courage, but you do not walk it alone. Walking in the Light does not shame you; it **reveals and heals**.

Wisdom Spiritual Insight

To master yourself, you must make peace with your whole self, not just the parts that you like, but also the parts that you are still learning to trust and grow. Your shadow is not a flaw in your faith; it's a doorway to deeper freedom.

When you accept your darkness, by choosing to walk in the Light, you step into love that drives out fears, love that's more powerful than shame, and overcome darkness.

You don't need to be afraid of what's hidden.

You only need to believe that Light is greater than your darkness.

Wisdom Spiritual Practice: Walking with Your Shadow in the Light
- **Create space for honesty.** In prayer or journaling, ask: *What am I avoiding within myself? What needs healing, not hiding?*

- **Invite God into your hidden places.** Say aloud: *"Shine Your light on anything I have kept in darkness."*
- **Practice self-compassion.** Speak to yourself with understanding, empathy, kindness, truth, and with love. Self-love is self-compassion, a nurturing force that guides you through the healing process and reminds you that you are worthy of love and care. **Seek support when needed.** Seeking safe communities and wise counsel are often part of the process.

Wisdom Reflection Prompts
- What wounds am I still carrying?
- Who or what do I need to forgive?
- What does my inner child need from me today?

Wisdom Exercises
- **Write a Letter to Yourself, or Persons from your past you want to release:** Write a letter to someone (alive or not) expressing all you've held in. You can burn or bury it to release the past.
- **Inner Child Visualization:** Close your eyes and imagine hugging your 7-year-old self. What do they say? What do you say back?

Wisdom Reflection Questions
1. What part of yourself have you been afraid to face or share?
2. What beliefs or behaviors have you adopted that no longer align with your healed self?
3. How would your life change if you stopped being afraid or judging your shadow and started healing it?

Wisdom Spiritual Declaration

I choose love and compassion. I commit to healing my life with faith. I declare healing for my hidden wounds. I open my heart to Light. I am loved, I am safe, I am whole and complete.
As you declare this powerful affirmation, you are affirming your commitment to healing and self-acceptance, affirming your worth and your ability to heal.

NOTES

Chapter Six

Surrender, Let Go, and Trust

The Sixth Step: Releasing Control and Resting in Faith

Spiritual self-mastery is not about gaining more control; it is about learning to let go. After embracing awareness, inner peace, alignment, and healing your shadow, **surrender** is the deepest act of trust. Embracing surrender is not a sign of giving up, but a **conscious choice** to hand over control. Surrender is an invitation to stop striving in your strength and start resting in divine strength, a strength that comes from your Faith and connection with God. Resting in divine strength involves releasing your grip on outcomes, expectations, and timing, and entrusting them to God's perfect plan. It's the bridge that leads you from where you are to where God is taking you.

Let Go and Embrace Your Becoming

You are an exquisite masterpiece. As you embrace your becoming, you honor your journey of growth, transformation, and the unfolding of your highest self. You learn from life's detours and breakthroughs, shaping your character and revealing your purpose, as becoming is the continuous process of self-discovery, growth, and development. Release the pressure to figure everything out and trust the process. Your becoming means accepting as well as celebrating the ups and downs of life in all its changes, imperfections, and embracing the process, seeing progress as success. It's recognizing that every step, especially the uncertain ones, is part of the divine plan for

your life. In this space of surrender and self-love, you allow your true self to emerge with grace, power, and authenticity, recognizing you are a work in progress. You are a *living process; r*elease and surrender the pressure to arrive at a specific destination. Celebrate your ongoing personal growth, the stumbles, the breakthroughs, the silent victories, the inner shifts no one sees. It's your divine unfolding, the becoming of who you are.
Align your Inspired Actions with Authenticity Authentic living looks like living your truth. Integrity is doing what aligns with your soul, not what pleases others.

Love is the language of Faith.

Love is the language of Faith because it is the purest expression of what we believe and who we trust. Faith is how we live, how we forgive, and how we extend grace. Love gives Faith its breath, making it visible through acts of kindness, compassion, and sacrifice. To walk in Faith is to speak in love, for love is the evidence of what is the unseen truth deeply known. When love becomes the language of our Faith, fear loses its grip, hope finds its wings, and the Divine presence is made manifest in and through us.

Why Is Surrender So Difficult?
Because we fear what we cannot see.
Because we've learned that control equals safety.
Because letting go feels like losing safety, when in truth, it reveals to us our divine power.
The false self resists surrender because it fears vulnerability. The spirit welcomes surrender because it knows the truth. *Trust the One who cares for you.*

What Surrender Looks Like in Practice

- **Releasing the need to figure it all out.** You can stop trying to control every outcome.
- **Letting go of "how" and "when."** Peace comes from trusting the process.
- **Laying down the weight of worry.** When anxiety arises, choose to speak Faith instead of fear.
- **Opening your heart.** Allow, surrender, and trust.

Surrender doesn't mean life gets easy. It means you stop resisting the flow of grace. You allow God to lead without needing constant evidence or proof. You let go and allow peace to take the place of pressure. It's a relief from the burden of control and a lightning of your spirit, bringing a sense of liberation and unburdening.

Wisdom Spiritual Insight

Your surrender leads to **spiritual elevation**. When you let go of fear, you step more fully into Faith. When you release your plan, you trust that truth will be revealed to you. When you stop focusing on the closed door, you start seeing the opportunities assigned to you. Letting go is not losing; it's freedom. Freedom to become who you are. Surrender is the **wisdom** of trusting the One who sees, who knows, and holds the whole plan. Your part is to *believe*, release, and receive.

Wisdom Spiritual Practices for Daily Surrender and Trust

- **Begin the day with this prayer:** *"God, I release what I cannot control. I trust you with what I cannot see."*
- **Write down what you're holding onto.** Then pray and symbolically release each item into God's hands.

- **Practice breath prayers.** Inhale and say: *"I let go."* Exhale and say: *"I trust You."*
- **End each day with reflection and creation:** *What did I carry today that I was to trust God to handle? What truth can I meditate on to create the outcome I desire?*

Wisdom Reflection Prompts

- Where in my life am I pretending or people-pleasing?
- What boundaries do I need to set?
- What does alignment feel like in my body?

Wisdom Exercises

- **Yes/No Audit:** For one week, only say "yes" to what aligns with your goals. Journal the results.
- **Authenticity Checklist:** Write three daily actions that make you feel true to yourself.

Wisdom Reflection Questions

1. What am I still trying to control that God is asking me to surrender?
2. How would my life feel if I truly trusted God's divine timing and plan?
3. What does surrender look like in this current season of my life?

Wisdom Spiritual Declaration

I surrender. I let go, and I trust my becoming. I release my fears, timelines, expectations, and control. I walk forward in peace, with an open heart. I trust and believe that all things are working for my highest good. I trust God's divine plan and divine timing. My trust empowers me to face the unknown with confidence, making me feel secure.

NOTES

Chapter Seven

Unity of Oneness

The Seventh Step: Living from Wholeness

The culmination of spiritual self-mastery is Wholeness, the sacred awareness that all is connected, all is divine, and all is One. **Oneness** is a transformative experience of seeing yourself through the lens of love, rather than separation. It's a level of consciousness where you transcend labels, borders, and the illusion of separation. Instead, you embrace the divine thread that unites **every soul**, every moment, every breath, in a state of profound Oneness. You are part of a larger whole, connected to every living being. Oneness is the return to your original spiritual design: union with God, harmony with others, and peace within yourself.

What Oneness Feels Like
- **You feel compassion even for those who hurt you, because you see their pain.**
- **You move from judgment to mercy because you realize we are all in process.**
- **You forgive more easily because you understand that holding onto hurts only hurts you more.**
- **You live with humility because you know that the same divine Spirit that guides you lives in others.**

Oneness is to live, lead, love, and serve from the awareness that love is all, and *we are one, which is a sign of becoming.*

From Separation to Sacred Belonging

The ego builds walls; the Spirit builds bridges.
The world teaches comparison; the Spirit teaches compassion.
Division is the language of fear; **Love is the language of faith**.
When you embrace unity and Oneness, you stop reacting to life with superiority or inferiority. Instead, you become a channel of healing. You carry peace wherever you go because you see yourself in others and others in yourself, made in the image of God.

Spiritual Practice for Cultivating Unity Consciousness and Align inspired Actions with Authenticity
Once you know who you are, you must live accordingly. Integrity is the daily practice of authenticity.
- Speak your truth, even when your voice shakes
- Set boundaries that protect your peace
- Say no to what is not aligned
- Say yes to what makes your soul expand

Small, courageous choices lead to lasting transformation.

Building Discipline and Devotion

Moving from separation to sacred belonging is a journey of reconnecting with your true self, with others, and with the Divine. It requires more than inspiration; it calls for discipline and devotion. Discipline is a commitment to show up through consistent practices that align with your values and vision. Devotion takes actions with intention, transforming routine into a ritual. Spiritual integrity, cultivated through discipline and dedication, dissolves the illusion of isolation and reawakens your sense of Oneness. Within this space of sacred belonging, you no longer strive to prove your worth; you embody it, living as a vessel of divine connection, purpose, and grace. Spiritual self-mastery is a sacred commitment to yourself and your becoming. You become who you are by showing up *consistently* with intention.

Creating routines that transform into rituals, like:
- Prayer or Stillness in the morning
- Movement that energizes your body
- Daily reflection and accountability

Discipline is not punishment. It is devotion to your evolution.

- **Practice seeing the divine in others.** In silence or prayer, look at someone and repeat inwardly, *"The light of God is in you."*
- **Release judgment quickly.** When it arises, pause and ask: *"What might this person be going through that I can't see?"*
- **Create moments of connection.** Smile, listen, and be fully present when interacting with yourself or others. Every act of love is a step toward unity.

You don't become who you are by wishing. You become who you are through sacred commitment.

Wisdom Spiritual Insight

It is unity consciousness when you honor your differences without division, and uniqueness without superiority. In this space, you begin to understand that (whatever you do, you do to yourself). (A Jamaican proverb).

You are not separate. You are one with God. *Only believe and you will begin to see yourself in God, God in yourself and God in everyone.*

Wisdom Reflection Prompts
- What am I most committed to right now?
- Where am I lacking consistency?

- What does devotion mean to me?
- How have I already grown?
- What am I still learning to love about myself?
- What does "becoming" mean to me?

You are a masterpiece and a work in progress. Don't rush your transformation.

Wisdom Exercises

- **Daily Devotion:** Create a habit tracker. Include spiritual, mental, and physical practices.
- **Morning Power Ritual:** Establish a morning practice that centers you before the world pulls you in.
- **Reflection Progress:** Compare a journal entry from 6 months ago to now. Highlight the transformation.
- **Affirmation Creation:** Write your own "I am becoming" statement, speak it daily.
- **Self-Declaration Ceremony:** Light a candle. Read aloud:

I honor my truth. I walk in my power. I choose to live aligned, awakened, and free. I am becoming more of who I am.

Wisdom Reflection Questions

1. Where in my life do, I still feel separated from God or myself?
2. How can I cultivate the habit of seeing others through the lens of Oneness and compassion?
3. What would change if I truly believed that all life connects through divine love?

Wisdom Spiritual Declaration

Today, I open my eyes and heart to Oneness. I see the Divine in myself and others. Love is my divine nature and divine language. I walk in unity, rooted in Spirit, and led by compassion for myself and others.

You are Transforming from BECOME to BECOMING to BEING!

Remember, transforming from BECOME to BECOMING is growth, expansion, and Spiritual self-mastery. Release the pressure of perfection and embrace progress, knowing that your becoming is not a destination, it is your divine path unfolding.

Once you've embraced the process of becoming, you step into the stillness and power of simply **BEING**. It is a state of alignment with your divine essence. It's about living as your authentic self without striving, proving, or performing. In **BEING**, becoming finds its fulfillment, and you rest in the freedom of wholeness.

NOTES

Conclusion

You are not chasing transformation—you are living the embodiment of it!
Now, it's time to **BE**.

You began this journey searching for clarity, strength, and purpose. Along the way, you discovered something greater—you already carried it all within you. You have reclaimed your **IDENTITY**—the unshakable truth of who you are. You have chosen to **BELIEVE**—to anchor your life in that truth until it shapes your vision, your choices, and your destiny. Now, you are **BECOMING** and living as the fullest expression of the masterpiece you are.

It's not the end. Self-mastery is not a finish line—it is a daily practice of **BEING**. Each sunrise presents another opportunity to realign with your truth, deepen your Belief, and embody your becoming in every thought, word, and action. There will be moments when the old voices try to return, in whispers of fear, doubt, or unworthiness. When they come, remember: they are not your voice. Your authentic voice speaks from a place of love, wisdom, and faith. Listen to that voice. You are not striving to be someone else—you are uncovering the fullness of who you've always been.

You are already the light, the vessel, the creation God designed. Now walk in it!
Live it! Not timidly, not halfway, but audaciously, courageously, boldly, beautifully, and unapologetically.
The world needs the truth of who you are, and only you can bring it.

Identity is Living to Your Divine Self and Your Highest Potential

Living to your Divine Self and your highest potential is a return to the truth of who you are. A life led by purpose, love, and guided by the wisdom that already lives within you. As you peel away the layers of fear, illusion, and limitation, you awaken to a power born from within. The path of spiritual self-mastery is where your choices align with your deepest values, and your actions reflect your divine essence. It is a journey of courage, growth, and grace. As you live from this elevated space, you transform your life and become a light that inspires others to rise to their highest truth.

Living to your highest potential is about awakening to the fullness of who you already are. It means rising each day with intention, embracing growth with humility, and aligning your actions with your deeper purpose. It is the ongoing choice to live authentically, courageously, and compassionately, even when the path is uncertain.

Realize your highest potential through self-awareness, self-belief, and soul-aligned, inspired action. It shows up in how you love, serve, create, and rise after every fall—cultivated in the quiet moments of reflection, resilience, and expressed in the bold steps you take toward your vision. To live to your highest potential is to honor your divine uniqueness, to move beyond fear, and to let your life be a testimony of what's possible when love, faith, purpose, and personal power align.

Through spiritual self-mastery, you move beyond awareness into embodiment. Learning not only to *embrace* truth, but to *live* it. You are now on the path of **self-actualization**, where your inner knowing transforms into conscious action, and your life becomes a living reflection of your highest self. Here, you make aligned choices with divine purpose, your gifts are shared freely, and love becomes the language through which you move in the world.

Believing is to trust. To become who you are is to answer that intentional invitation with courage and faith. To walk the path of spiritual self-mastery is to return, again, to the sacred truth that everything you need is already within. You are not becoming something you are not. You are remembering what has always been true. You are the light. You are the vessel. You are the miracle. Believe. Become who you are, and let your life speak for itself.

Transforming from IDENTITY to BELIEF! It is the awakening of who you are at your core and choosing to trust that truth.

Transforming from BELIEVE to BECOME! It is the courageous act of embodying that trust, allowing Belief to shape your actions and life.

Transforming from BECOME to BECOMING to BEING! Is the sacred unfolding where you shift from seeing yourself as a finished product, to embracing growth as a continual journey, and finally resting in the wholeness of simply living as your true self.

Together, these transformations form the pathway of spiritual self-mastery: awakening your **Identity**, strengthening your **Belief**, stepping into your **Becoming**, and embodying your **Being.**

You have walked through seven sacred steps on the path of spiritual self-mastery, not to become someone else, but to **remember who you truly are**. This journey was never about striving or perfection. It was always about awakening, surrendering, and returning to the divine truth within you.

Through every chapter, there is truth: **Believe** that you are not alone in your transformation. Believe that God is not distant; He is within you, guiding, healing, and speaking. Believe that your highest self is not a future destination; it is who you are now. This guide will not give you all the answers. It is to help you become more aware, listen more deeply to the voice of truth, so you can change your beliefs and initiate the transformation of becoming.

Accept the invitation to embody your awareness, walk in peace, release control, embrace your fullness and wholeness, and trust the divine design of your life. Let your life be the evidence of your Belief. What you believe will always move you to act. Let your Spirit lead because Spirit is your Identity. Let love guide every step because love is who you are. When your path feels uncertain, when fear whispers louder than faith, return to the still small voice within and remember: You don't have to have it all figured out. You don't have to be perfect. Only believe, and return to yourself, and walk the path of spiritual self-mastery: TO REMEMBER WHO YOU ALREADY ARE. You are already enough. You are already whole. Now, live from that TRUTH.

Wisdom Final Affirmation

I am a divine creation, deeply connected to God and all things. I walk in peace, purpose, and power. I embrace all of who I am with grace and love. I surrender, and I live with an open heart.

A Letter for Embodying Who You Are

Remember, Darely, Beloved.

You are Already Who You Are Becoming.
If these words have found you, it is not by chance; it is by divine guidance. Somewhere within, you have heard truth calling you home to yourself. The voice that says, *"You are more than enough. You are ready now."*

IDENTITY*! A SPIRITUAL SELF-MASTERY GUIDE* is your awakening, a spiritual roadmap for you if you are ready to rise above fear, doubt, and limitation. It speaks to your desire to live in alignment with truth and divine purpose. You are here to transform your experience to live to your highest potential. We must heed the call to return inward to the sacred stillness of the soul, remembering who we truly are.

I want you to know you are not lost. You are on the right path. Every moment has led you to this place, even the ones wrapped in pain, have guided you toward this awakening. Your becoming is not a destination. It is the unfolding of what has always been true.

You are already whole. Let go of the shackles of expectations, limitations, doubts, and fears dictating who you are and who you should be. Embrace the freedom of self-leadership. You are already worthy, beloved. The approval of others or your achievements does not determine your worth. It is an inherent part of your being, a divine gift that you carry within you. You are already the light you seek. Your inner radiance and your unique gifts and talents are ready to shine brightly.

On your journey of discovering your identity, belief, and becoming, you will experience days of truth and days when your false self, challenges you. Honor them and let your faith be the bridge between where you are now and who you are becoming. When doubt visits, remember: Belief is choosing truth over fear. When resistance rises, remember: Becoming is about living in alignment with who you are.

You already know the way. Reflect deeply. Commit faithfully. Your heart is already fluent in love. Live your life from the perspective of 'IDENTITY'. Let truth be your guiding light, your source of strength, and your anchor in turbulent storms. Whether you are just beginning your spiritual journey or deepening an existing one, cultivate spiritual self-mastery.

Believe in your divine potential. You are strong enough to carry the vision that is within you. Walk forward with grace. Trust the unfolding. Embrace it and let it empower you.

P.S. Remember, **you are not becoming someone else. You are REMEMBERING who you already are.**

Poem: *WHO I AM*

I am Spirit,
I possess a soul,
I live in this body.

Despite rejection and abandonment,
I held a secret beauty within me,
of resilience.
Through loneliness and doubt,
I carried a hidden strength.
Through seasons of struggle and wondering,
I stood firm and resilient.

I was forged.
I was never ugly.
I was not forgotten.
I was waiting.
I was not what they named me.
I was not what they saw.

Spirit unveiled,
the truth uncovered,
the beauty that was within me all along.

When you see me,
You see yourself:
becoming, awakening,
rising into who You already are.

At last, Spirit revealed me.

By Sopheia McMorris

NOTES

Next Steps

To find out more, visit website:
https://sopheiaspeakswisdom.com/

Or contact me via email at:
sopheia@sopheiaspeakswisdom.com
https://sopheiaspeakswisdom.com/

About the Author

Sopheia McMorris is an Executive Wisdom Mentor and founder of *Wisdom Speaks Life*. Her journey into self-mastery began through personal trials that revealed a life-changing truth: *Identity is the single most powerful force shaping our experiences and success.*

With warmth and deep insight, Sopheia shares her wisdom to help seekers and leaders reconnect with their true selves, release limiting beliefs, and step into lives of purpose and abundance. Her mindset philosophy has impacted family, friends, clients, and professionals worldwide, guiding them from struggle to empowerment through a simple yet transformative process.

A graduate with a Bachelor of Science degree in African American Studies and Political Science, and with more than 20 years of teaching and mentoring experience, Sopheia has become a trusted voice in the field of self-mastery. Through international speaking engagements, workshops, and online media, she continues to inspire people to awaken to their divine identity and boldly create lives they love.

Her mission is clear: to remind others that they are already whole, worthy, and called to greatness.

"You are not becoming someone else. You're remembering who you already are."
—Sopheia McMorris

Endnotes

Identity is Truth. Your most authentic identity is not something you create; it is something you awaken to. It is already within you, waiting for you to claim it. **Your journey is Ongoing** – Spiritual self-mastery is not a destination but a continual unfolding. Every experience, every challenge, and every moment is an invitation to live more deeply in your truth. This ongoing nature of the journey keeps you engaged and committed to your personal development.

Love is Your Foundation – No transformation can last if it is not rooted in Love, and built on Love, for yourself, others, and the Divine source that sustains all life. Self-discovery and spiritual growth create a secure foundation for **Faith to Empower Identity** – Believing in who you are is the bridge between awakening and embodiment. Faith is the key that turns your identity from a mere idea into a lived reality. **Integration is key** to healing, wholeness, and authenticity, which requires embracing all parts of yourself—the light, the shadow, and the spaces in between.

Your Life is Your Legacy – Every choice you make affirms or denies your true self. Live in alignment with your highest identity, and your life will become a testimony of divine truth.
You Are Not Alone – The path of spiritual self-mastery is personal but never solitary. God walks with you, and your healing ripples outward, touching the lives of others. Divine presence is not just a guide, but a constant companion on your spiritual journey.

Identity Leads to Belief, to Becoming, to Being – This guide is not an ending but a beginning. As you embrace your identity, may it lead you to deeper faith, greater

courage, and the next step in your spiritual self-mastery
journey.

NOTES

NOTES

NOTES

2

Ancestry

The younger man followed me out of the room. Looking back, I realized it was a classroom thinking now to myself how annoying this guy is. I turned around to try and get rid of him but stopped in my tracks.

Rosealine: Who are you?

He replied to

Dark Voice: very funny Rosealine you fell asleep in class again. You also started shouting random things...... Ex was it? .....

The young man gave me a very strange look and an incredibly soft kiss on the cheek.

Dark Voice: He chuckled you spoke about a path, lights and people.

Now I was suffocating, really needing to get out of here. As I reached the glass doors, I pushed the doors open, turned to say bye, and fell onto the railing. I began to fall down the stairs. All I kept thinking was how Familiar this all is. Kinda like Deja vie. When I almost hit my face a strong set of arms caught me. Pulling my body into an upright position. Once I got my balance, I looked over. It was him it was Ex. Exavier my Exavier. How could I have forgotten this moment? You saved me from a nasty black eye right before graduation and that young man was Travis. Man, he had such a crush on me back then. Which made him really hate you.

But since you are here and so much younger this had to be a dream. I closed my eyes tightly at this point and then just like that our life together played like a movie, every memory every touch. Like walking on stage announcing our school choices. Our first date at that cute little diner back in our hometown. You know the small towns in Alabama called Auburn, such a tiny place. Population of 63,973 people.

We are hours from home now though. California has such a different lifestyle. As the memories kept playing on it was like I was there again. Falling in love with you all over again. Why is this happening to me? Finally, it all came to a halt. When I opened my eyes, I was back in the dark tomb. I continued walking and realized I' am barefoot and the floor of the tomb was rough. It felt like base-rock under my feet.

Up ahead was a stick of fire, it is called a torch maybe. As I pulled it down, I saw pictures on the side of the walls beside me. I tried to read it, but it was in calligraphy and chiseled drawings. Feeling it with my fingers it was rough having a groove like texture. This had to be from my ancestors.

Egyptians sure had a way of storytelling. What I could make out from all of it was what looked like a pharaoh and the details of his burial. Unfortunately, my mother Clarissa did not teach me much about our ancestry. She died when I was only a baby. But that is a story for another time. So not really a chance for me to really know what it was saying. After staring in fascination, I found something new that caught my eye.

It was like a full-on life-size pharaoh. This was amazing, the craftmanship alone was astonishing. Jewels for the eyes and what looked like diamonds around the head piece. As I traced my hands along the gold body of the pharaoh. My eyes met back to the red ruby jeweled eyes. Looking deep into them I started to see a figure leaning closer. Suddenly I could see what looked like a fallen pharaoh. He was walking towards me, it seemed almost zombie like. By the way I hate horror movies.

Rosealine: Wake up! Rosealine wake up!

I screamed to try and snap me out of this dream like state. Now I closed my eyes and then a voice entered my mind. I knew this voice, Ex! Finally, Ex.

I could hear him anywhere; it is as if my soul was attached to him. Quickly I opened my eyes but no Ex, he was not here.

Rosealine: Ex!

As I called out to him, I started to cry. But suddenly a hand touched my shoulder. Jumping back ready to fight whoever it was who invaded my personal space. Looking up I could see it was the pharaoh from before he was now in front of me....

Now he was lifelike, he smiled such a sly boyish smile. He spoke to me with such elegance and authority.

Pharaoh: Rosealine so nice to finally meet you. Your birth was such a blessing to my family.

What was he talking about?.......Who was he...... why would I be so important to him or his family? I cut him off mid-sentence.

Rosealine: who are you!!! What are you talking about?

He silenced me with a simple wave of his hand. Interrupting me while I was asking him questions.

Pharaoh: Listen Rosealine everything will be clear in time but right now you have a choice to make and extraordinarily little time to make it.

What he said was very confusing to me. What choice? What time? All these questions flew through my mind, but no answers followed. My anxiety kicked in an my heart it began to race. He spoke softly now.

Pharaoh: Rosealine everything that happens in life happens for a reason. It is what we call fate.... Do you agree with what I am telling you?

Before I could finish processing what he just said to me my mouth blurted out
Rosealine: Yes!
My mind finished the sentence of course everything happens for a reason. He shook his head in agreement. Then he pointed to the wall where there was another set of drawings carved into the tomb.
Pharaoh: The choice is now yours as it has been before. From century to century.
Rosealine: This does not make sense please tell me more be more implicit.
Pharaoh: You have little time so please hurry before it is too late.

I walked over to the wall scanning the images and turned to ask him what this meant but he had gone, I could no longer see him. The young pharaoh was back resting. What did he mean by.... "What Choices?........

3

Choice or Ultimatums

osealine: Ouch!

My head had begun to hurt and sweat. Water dripping from my face. This was odd for me. I 'am not one to sweat I've always been extremely active. The anxiety was really getting to me as I walked in the cold tomb my body was on fire. Reaching out to the walls I began to feel extremely ill my stomach was turning.

Again, racing thoughts of what choices I could have. I 'am dead right... I would have to be. Touching the wall with fingertips desperately trying to interpret what I was feeling. But with my mind so clouded it was even harder looking more in depth at the wall I did see a young girl in the pictures. Guessing from the pictures, she was pregnant as I went down the wall further in time, she was giving birth to her baby. But in the pictures, something very disturbing happened. These non-life-like cold dark hands. They were reaching down and taking her soul from her body as she gave birth to her child right when her child took her first breath. I took a moment and fought back the tears coming to my eyes.

As I make it further down the wall a dark figure now appears the women who now appears hallow is at his feet begging. The fig-

ure raises his hand and points to a set of scrolls. When I followed the figures hand, I noticed a set of scrolls setting out. I knew I had to now read the scrolls to figure this all out. Picking up the yellow incredibly old and fragile scroll, I started to read as I rolled it out across the tomb floor. As I read it three times over it was explaining the meaning of life. I pondered the saying until it clicked it was her life or her child's life. Is this the choice I am being given? Then everything came flooding back into my head. The accident showing how badly I got hurt and me passing out. Not waking up to Destiney or Ex but in a tomb. I died and now the choice is in my hands this all made sense. Ex was yelling at me to wake up as I tried to respond but he could never hear me. If you are a mother, then you know the choice you would make. The sacrifice you would make. Could you do this?

As the choice bubbled up into my throat, I felt weak, my heart was slowing, the time was coming to a halt. I love Ex with all my heart, but I knew he would be strong for Destiney and so it is her the choice is her. I 'am choosing my baby girl!

I would never live with myself if Destiney was to die a life for a life. I got to my feet and yelled at the top of my lungs, not sure at whom I was yelling.

Rosealine: You get me, you can have me! Let my daughter live! I will choose her every time.

Before I could get another word to leave my lips, he appeared not the pharaoh from before but a tall dark figure. He was dark and gave me an uneasy feeling. Should I be afraid? This was him from the wall Anubis the Egyptian god of death. He was a dark hollow figure, the one taking the women's soul. This must mean he is here to collect ill become just another hollow body six feet under. Anubis is tall and mysterious. Extremely gorgeous, you *would have to be blind not to see how inviting he looks. The fear left my body and for no reason even the darkness of the tomb no longer bothered me. He started to speak, his tone so dead and dry.*

Anubis= Rosaeline you are mine at last

Before I could even speak my soul was hovering over my lifeless body that now lay still on the tomb floor.
Rosealine:Why Am' I here I made my choice I chose Destiney. But something caught my attention.

<u>*Time changes......*</u>

Ex he was crying over my body lying in a hospital bed. His head was on my chest, his hand holding mine. This is when I realized I could not even feel him anymore, not even his tears hitting my chest or his hand holding mine.

My heart ached for what I had taken for granted all those years. Pulling my eyes away from this so I would not feel regret for the choice I just made. Turning my face now, I saw her the most beautiful little girl. Instantly I went to hold her or just feel her in my arms. Her skin is so soft and that perfect complexion. My Egyptian tan and Exavier's gorgeous eyes. She was an angel wrapped in a perfectly pink blanket. One I had looked for over and over to find.

Her hazel eyes were looking right through me it killed me knowing I could never actually hold her. But I knew I made the right choice. Looking back at Ex I knew he would move on he would just have to forgive me. Ex would move on pull his life together Destiney and he would actually have a life to live. I would never regret giving her life. Fate is a cruel beast and karma really is a witch. This felt like only merely seconds but I could feel something pulling at my soul.... Yanking me away from the life I had known and wanted for so long.

<u>Time changes....</u>

Anubis drew me back to the tomb once more. I was a wreck how could I gain and lose what was meant to be mine all in the same day all at the same time. Anubis broke through my emotions and told me in his deep dry tone that he had something to offer me a deal to present to me. Anubis and I sat down on the tomb floor and the conversation began.

Anubis= Rosealine

His voice now radiated with power and confidence it was as if it was gripping my soul.

Anubis= From here on out the choice you make will define what happens to your soul. Will I keep your soul or will I let it wonder....

Am 'I really dead?... you really reached into my body taking my soul.

Anubis=Rosealine pay attention, yes, I'm the god of death normally I reach in and retrieve a soul, and it became mine to deal with but with you.... Well, you have options.

What could that mean options......

Anubis= Rosealine the pharaoh you met before he was once in your shoes and had what I like to call abilities that you also possess.

Rosealine: Hold on Anubis you must have the wrong girl the only ability I have is to be able to walk one foot in front of the other. Let me tell you that is not something to brag about.

He chuckled loudly it was deep and dark. His lips made a rough sound, his Toung almost sounded more like a hiss. This creature was dark, there was not a drop of light in him or around him he radiated evil.

Anubis= Rosealine do you honestly believe that everything that just happened to you was merely an accident let me be the first if only to tell you that will never be true. Nothing that happens to you is accidental. This is fate.

Rosealine: Wait! Are you saying that everything I just went through is fate! Losing the two people I love the most Ex and Destiney is what you call fate.

Anubis= Rosealine!

My name flew out as a growl.

Anubis= Do not ever raise your voice or change your tone to me. Do you understand me gifted or not I do not except disrespect. I do not need you, soon you will see you need me.

My mind began to wonder fate this word sickened me and gifted abilities oh please. This all sounded completely absurd. Ex my gorgeous Exavier a flash back to him rubbing my stomach smiling and telling me that soon I would find pure happiness. Be-

ing a mom is something I would be perfect at, no one can take that away from me. Even when I was stressed or scared, he could still make me laugh. The flashback was short lived. A big dark huff came out of Anubis' mouth.

Rosealine:Fine Anubis please tell me why I need you...?

Anubis= Lets start by me telling you what I want. I'm in need of a new Tailor of Time and I can offer you the chance to see Ex and Destiney over the course of time.

Rosealine: Wait hold on Anubis what do you mean see them like, I get to see them in person?

My heart was filled with joy.

Rosealine: Name your price Anubis.

Anubis= Being a Tailor of Time is like being a superhero of sorts except I pull the strings. You already can go back in time and alter the outcome. The only way you can use this ability is if I let your soul wonder. I can give you the chance to be able to go back to your time and see Destiney grow into the women she is going to be. Let you at least be a part of her in some small way or you can be yet another soul I hold on to and you will never see life again. But like you have said everything in life or in death has a price. Nothing comes free.

Rosealine: Yes, but Anubis could I see them every day?

Anubis= Yes Rosealine what I offer to you is simple you do as I say and go back in time and change Peoples's lives by also taking people's lives.

Rosealine: I would be killing people.

I was horrified by what I just heard, could I really take a life just so I could selfishly watch what could have been my life? .... Unfortunately, yes, I want to see Destiney become a woman.

Anubis= Now Rosealine the price you must pay is simple.

Rosealine: Wait it's not killing people for you? Thats not the price I am paying?

Anubis= Stop saying it that way you are giving someone else a chance to live by taking something as simple as a life. You must stop looking at this as a negative and think positive. This is the circle of life, so it has no real benefit to me, it is not giving me something that I do not already get or have.   Your price is you will be mine.

My body froze I was stiff and unable to move the more it echoed through my mind repeatedly My body started to tingle as the word rolled of my Toung. He chuckled that deep dark laugh.

Anubis= Rosealine you know what I want now so do we have a deal?

Nothing left my lips, not a sound or a single breath.

Anubis= Rosealine you are the most beautiful and pure hearted creature I have ever met or had the chance to touch and hold in my grasp. Just think what I can give you immortality a life after death.

Rosealine: It is not as simple as just giving you my heart Anubis it already belongs to........Ex

Anubis= Oh yes Exavier is it...... I knew he would become a problem, let me make that issue nonexistent for you. Picture this before you speak if you choose to deny me now. I will take this offer completely off the table, you will merely be a soul floating alongside all the others. Nothing more than a distant memory. Without you here who will watch over that weak pathetic mortal you love? The family you left behind. Who will be here to control my rage and very vengeful ego? Just know Rosealine I do not take rejection well. I ALWAYS GET WHAT I WANT!

Rosealine: Anubis please why can't I just be your Tailor of Time and do your bidding? I can collect the souls of your choosing, and you let me love who I love?

Anubis= Rosealine no one said you had to love me I simply said I want your heart I want you! So, for the last time will you be mine? Quickly speak Rosealine you ae running out of time because I 'am running out of patience. Decide or seal your fate.

At this moment Destiney came to my mind. I want to see her grow her first step her first words. The first time she falls and gets back up. I want to see her beautiful face will she look like me? Ex... yes Ex I want to know that he forgave me and that he is doing well and living his life. Just seeing his face would be enough. I cannot disappear completely, not right now, not with so much unfinished business lingering. Anubis turned and started to walk off.

Rosealine: Anubis wait!

Anubis= What Rosealine I'm very busy. I do not have time for your pathetic mortal unpleasant habits to get in the way. You either surrender yourself to me or you suffer alone in silence for-

ever. I told you I will not ask again Rosealine. The choice is now yours.......

Rosealine: Anubis I............

4

Forever

Rosealine: Fine I will do it.......

Anubis= Do what Rosealine

Rosealine: I will do what you want.

Anubis= Say it then Rosealine Tell me what I want. Say it, Rosealine!

His snarl sounded like nails on a chalk board. However, I knew what he wanted, he wanted me to say the words that would feel like acid on my lips burning me from the inside out.

Rosealine: I will be yours Anubis You can have me.

Those words felt sour bitter coming off my Toung it was regret. Now I felt it I just gave my heart my soul and my body over to Anubis the god of death. A dark immortal monster. He smiled such a dark smile giving my body chills and made me cringe. He was now walking towards me. I felt scared at this moment I was never going to be able to get free of him. This would be forever...... The closer he got the colder I felt the sicker I felt. I thought to my-

self because my mind was all that I had left that was only mine. Ex what have I done...... this came off my lips as a whisper.

Rosealine: Exavier Jones and Destiney Jones I love you forever and always until my last breath leaves my chest.

Anubis now had his ice-cold hand on my cheek running his fingers across my face and into my hair. His gaze was harsh, and I could see the pride in his eyes he got what he wanted. My mind felt so lost and so gone.

Then emotions I felt kept coming in waves. His touch physically hurt me. His strength just in one fingertip was like power I could never imagine. He made me so nervous I felt so out of control witch I really hate.

Anubis grabbed my face and leaned in and kissed me. I tried so hard to pull away from him, but his hands held me in place. Anubis was rough and forceful, nothing like Ex. The feeling that took over once I gave in it was electric, it made my entire body tingle. I was so weak He spoke to me so gentle now.

Anubis= The gift I told you about is now active in your body. You should be feeling the effects shooting through your body. With this gift you will now be able to go back in time and change the fate of others. I will warn you. You CANNOT alter your own life, only the lives of others. If you do not choose to listen, you will end up erasing your entire family line. You can look as we agreed on, but you cannot touch interfering would be devastating. Do you understand? Rosealine? Do you hear me? ROSEALINE?

Rosealine: Yes, Anubis I understand. Why do you insist on yelling at me?

Anubis= You function as if you cannot hear me. I would not yell if you would show me that you hear me and respond when I have spoken to you. I will not have you ignore me. I 'am a god do not forget that.

Rosealine: You radiate arrogance in everything you say and do even in your walk. I cannot stand to be near you.

Anubis= Whatever you say Rosealine let us go over your rules now.

Rosealine: Rules? You never said I would have rules......

Anubis= Well you did not think you would just walk around and do as you please with no remorse...... Fate is not a game that you want to play around with. The world must equal out give and take. Your job is to provide options and second chances. Once a request has been made you will be carried off through time to the time zone of the individual. No, you are not a fairy god mother you do not grant wishes. You will find a way to insert yourself into this person's life. Before the tragic moment happens, you will give them a choice.

Rosealine: How will I know when and if this will happen?

Anubis= This is why I' am here Rosealine since I' am the keeper of the dead. When tragedy strikes, I see it all play through like a movie. When this happens, I will send you back to that time zone before the tragedy takes place. This will give you the edge you need to make this all happen smoothly. Now rule #1 A life for a life #2 You only get one chance #3 I make all final choices and decisions. #4 This is the hardest but most important one you cannot have emotion or empathy control your choice. Weakness is not tolerated in this line of work. Do we have an agreement do you understand?

Rosealine:Yes Anubis of course,

Honestly, I have no clue what all these rules mean. Or how they would even play out, However, I am not going to start questioning what he says. I will learn as it goes. Growing up I never could have expected such a turn of fate. The way I saw my life was a big family of two or three kids and a successful career with a retirement plan to be in the tropics. But instead, I will spend my remainder of whatever it is I have in a dark wet tomb. Guess fate had other plans not sure why, but I will find out.

Rosealine: Anubis, I cut the silence asking him how I can see Ex and Destiney.

Rosealine: What do I have to do to get to see them?

His face became cold, his eyes narrowed, I could tell this annoyed him.

Anubis: Rule #5 His name can never leave your lips again. Especially since they belong to me.

I immediately started to argue back but quickly silenced myself because all I wanted to do was see them. His expression cooled off as he began to explain to me how.

Anubis: When you should want to see Destiney all you need to do is close your beautiful eyes and make the request to me. I will keep my word and send you to her time wherever she is.

Before he could finish explaining I closed my eyes and thought of Destiney and her perfect face. Feeling the rush of energy and I was gone.

5

Crying

rying......I can hear a sweet cry ...Destiney.... Is that my baby girl?

I could not exactly tell because Anubis had taken me so fast, I never heard her scream or cry anything. I opened my eyes and there she was the most beautiful little girl the nurse was washing her off. Her perfect Carmel complexion those hazel green almond shaped eyes. She was alive and breathing. Looking at her in that moment would have been enough for me.

Then I felt him before he even entered the room, I could feel his hand on the small of my back. Of course, that was wishful thinking. I spoke to him as if he could hear me.

Look Exavier look what we made look at our beautiful daughter. I just kept pretending I was able to take this moment in with him laughing, talking and crying. Please forgive me, Ex I want you to know I'm doing this for you and Destiney for us. You would have never forgiven yourself and I would never forgive myself if I had let her die.

As we stood shoulder to shoulder the nurse handed our daughter to you, I knew I had made the right decision. I vowed I would never let anything happen to either one of you. She is safe and so are you. Now I can see the smile on your face and the tears running down your cheek. This was going to make you whole and fill your heart. I leaned in to kiss her soft cheek but then it hit me in the gut hard. Anubis was pulling me back to the tomb, my prison. My heart felt torn.

I wanted so bad for you to see me and know me Destiney. All these doubts came crashing down and into my brain. What if I never get to feel you is that enough for me. Can I except loving you from a far...... Exavier please take care of our baby girl as I left the time zone, I left those words hanging in the air.

Rosealine: I love you both no matter where I 'am.

Being back in this tomb was very depressing. I turned to Anubis.

Rosealine: Why wouldn't you let me kiss her just once!? Why did you pull me back so quickly????!!!!

Anubis=Rosealine I told you about your tone!

When he gets mad his eyes narrow his expression tenses up. I can honestly say it scares me.

Anubis= Listen Rosealine we must finish one last ritual this is the last step in you becoming mine. We must bind our hearts together.

Rosealine: I laughed and spoke softly you Anubis have a heart? What a joke you have no heart.

Anubis= Rosealine, listen to me I will not continue to argue with you or listen to this nonsense.

Rosealine: What if I changed my mind? You already activated my gift, for what do I need you? I can just go back in time and change everything starting with you. I can change you being here and who you are. I can make it to where you are never even born.

I could see his expression changing in anger, his eyes narrowing but I could not shut up, I kept going hit after hit. I knew I would never actually be able to do any of this. His anger kept rising before I knew it, his hands were around my neck pulling me up to him. But somehow, he did it gently and harshly but did not hurt me. I know this was him showing restraint because his eyes said something quite different. He leaned in and whispered in my ear.

Anubis: Rosealine if you do not shut those beautiful lips of yours, I will have no choice but to force you.

Shocked by his restraint I figured he would snap kill me harm me. But no, just a tight grip around my neck and a firm whisper. This scared me even more. But I did as he said and shut my mouth. He started to relax and clear his mind. This fight had been exhausting my body hit the tomb floor as he let go. I just laid there falling into a small sleep.

Rosealine: Anubis? Anubis......

nothing and no one, just me. Part of me wished this had all just been a nightmare and that I would wake up and Ex would be holding me. He would kiss me softly and tell me everything would be fine. He would say he loves me and would never let anything happen to me. Foolishly I would believe him.

That was when everything was simple and innocent. I should have loved harder and really showed him how much he meant to me all these years. I made myself rest now from my feelings and thoughts hoping to at least dream of you.

6

Awakened

*B*oom!

Crack!

The sounds of ruckus sent me into a panic.

What could that be? When I opened my eyes, I now saw I was no longer in the tomb, the place I had called safe. Never thought I could say safe, and tomb together or even miss it. This is when it hit me, I was time traveling once more. This no warning thing was not going to work for me. It felt like I was moving through the air carelessly. I didn't see, hear or feel anything. I barely could even move a muscle. My heart and mind racing trying to find anything to hold on to.

I was feeling weaker and weaker as this continued. Once it all stopped, I felt dizzy, a little lightheaded and very confused. I reached around as if I needed something to grab or touch. The only thing I noticed was how incredibly bright it all was. As I settled everything became calm and still. Then I thought he was very mad yesterday did he decide to just kill me. Is this what it feels like to be dead? Am I floating, falling, flying......

He must have meant it when he said he does not need me. But maybe I do need him...... Ugh I stopped myself from finishing this sentence. The thought of Destiney came into my mind. What if I never see her again? What if I messed it up? Thats what I always do is mess things up. Ex was the one who fixed things. I broke down.

Rosealine: Anubis! Anubis! No response Anubis!! Still nothing

I had to just lay here and soak my cheeks with tears. The longer I lay the more aware of the ground I became was this sand?... Is that sand? This took me back to a fond memory with my father. My father would always tell me stories of Egypt and how the sand felt beneath his toes. How warm the sun felt on his skin and how he loved the warmth it brought to his face.

This was nothing like that. I was very aware now that sand was in my hair and every crease of my body as if I were bathed in sand. I was now frustrated so I made myself get up. The sun I was feeling was not warm, I was freezing. My survival instincts had to kick in at some point, right? This was not going to stop me. The fact I could feel and see had to mean I was alive, right?

This was not going to stop me from seeing my baby girl. Now to figure out what has happened and move forward. So, step one shelter I need a place to be safe and warm. So far all I see is sand and more sand. But maybe if I start walking, I will come across something. This will be positive while I walk why not take in the scenery the freedom.

When I lived in the city you did not get to see things like this. The sun was setting, the stars barely shining. It was going to be dark soon. Blisters on my feet and no end in sight. My clothes looked like rags torn and faded. They were falling off me showing entirely too much skin for the condition I 'am in. Knowing my hair was a mess I reached up and began to braid it so that it was no longer in my face. I had not worn braids since middle school.

Never had the time and never really liked how my face looked. But desperate times call for desperate measures. The darker it got the stronger the breeze got the colder the night air felt. I had no water, no shelter and had been walking for hours. I had to survive the night, right? He would not let me just die out here......Finally I could see peeks from pyramids up ahead.

Safety finally I just needed to push a bit further. I made it to the pyramids and collapsed. I need water, I need food, shelter. I have never felt so alone. So far everything that has happened has been a challenge when is easy coming. This finally broke me. I did what I tell myself to never do. I cried. I cried so much that all I could taste was salt. Now I was red and puffy I am sure it was a big cry, but I felt almost relieved like I could keep going now. But that feeling of relief was short lived cause what happens next wasn't easy.....

Suddenly two sets of strong hands grab me from behind all I could do was scream for Ex to help me.

Rosealine: Help me Ex please Ex where are you?

I said this repeatedly until it hit me, he was not coming. All I have is me. My heart sank into my chest. I was scared, terrified. Who are they? What do they want? They threw me into a cage like an animal. Off we went as they pulled me on a cart displaying me for anyone to see. Bump after bump all I could think is why is this happening to me?

72 hours ago, I was going to be a mother and have my fairy-tale ending. This cannot be my story this cannot be all that will be written for me. I am weak, starved and alone, I am done for it is over. As we got closer, I saw a city ahead and I started to smell the scent of jasmine and lavender; it was calming for a moment. Also, a subtle change to the stench from the men. Once we got to the entrance of the city they stopped and began talking.

Of course, I did not really understand the words they spoke. It was Arabic their native Tonge. In California they did not even offer this as a language course. Even though I could not understand I kept saying the words back to myself as if not to forget,
Two Men: Sanakhudhuha illaa alqusr Alfireawn ymkn an yequarir madna yufealbuha (we will take her to the palace the pharaoh will decide what to do with her.) ahtaj iillaa manzil jaded zawjatan haha (I need a new housewife)

They spoke back and forth like this laughing and all I could do was sit and wait. Moments passed the wagon stopped and the men grabbed me out and threw me to the ground. How dare he...... But I was out of the cage.... My eyes glared at this man, this man who could treat me like I meant nothing. But as my glare hardened, he smiled.... As he smiled my face relaxed my glare had fallen into a blank expression. He let me stand with no arms to hold me and no chains to restrain me. Could it be finally a man with common sense.....

The more the men spoke back and forth the more my mind began to adapt and learn the language they were speaking. It is almost as if someone had put google translate into my brain. The two men who had taken me stopped talking turned and bowed to the nice-looking man, But way to full of himself king, that is why he acted and carried himself so differently.

I'd love to meet his Mama she did right when raising him. He spoke now with such power in his voice. Younger man. He was dark and mysterious but had a confident smirk on his face. As the two men stood, they called him King Ramesses. As I thought

Ramesses: Who have you brought to me in the middle of the night?

His tone changed to sharp, almost spiteful.

The Two men began to speak.

Two Men: We found this one lurking among your pyramids trying to break in your majesty.

The king turned to me looking me up and down his eyes narrowing a look that could kill. Now I knew I could be in trouble, no one ever looked at me so cross except my papa. He spoke with a firm voice.

Ramesses: You peasant girl, is this true were you looking to break into my pyramids?

I spoke up now my voice a little shaky, since he is a king in all.

Rosealine: No sir I was just trying to find shelter since I got lost. I was cold, the only thing around me was your pyramids. This was merely a mistake I only needed a place to sleep.

Ramesses: Where is your family, who is your father peasant. He is your provider. What is your title?
Family?

Rosealine: Sir my family has been gone a long time now, I'm Rosealine no title.

After the king pondered my response, he spoke with a much calmer tone.

Ramesses: You can come stay with my wife in the palace, she finds herself in need of a little help. You seem to be no threat to me, or my kingdom please follow.

As we started to walk up the steps of his palace, I noticed how easy it was to understand the words he spoke. But the crazy part was he was understanding me.... Do I now speak Arabic? All I am thinking is I am grateful for this odd experience; it saved me for the night. Then it hit me this is the gift the gift Anubis had spoken about. Finally, something he gave me has paid off. So many questions floating in my head unanswered.

My biggest question at present why am 'I here.....
Once we made it up the stairs of the palace, he turned to look at me. Really looking me over... made me feel kind of ew... But what he said made me feel even more ew.

Ramesses: You girl you look horrible the desert has not been good to you. I can't have you meet my wife smelling and looking like that. Go wash in the helps quarters and once you have finished my wife will be waiting.

Well, this was a twist in time am I really enslaved by a dead pharaoh.... I cannot decide laugh or cry. Never could I have seen this coming, I walked over to the water laid out for me, it was cold and so was I. The red clay did not help the getting clean part but still it was better than how I had been. To say I missed home was an understatement.

My nice hot bath with my soothing oils, my one-hundred-dollar luffa and all the bubbles in the world taking away the worries of the days. Getting lost in those nice safe memories could only hold me for so long, reality came shortly after. Surely you are thinking this can't get worse, but you'd be wrong, here comes the air drying.

But after the much deserved in my mind pity party. I got myself dressed and headed to her quarters. I have never had to help a queen before. Also, fun fact for you all readers Egyptians bathe in a coed style talk about modesty going out the window and embarrassment setting in.

While I looked around the place as I walked to her quarters, I saw statues and how the palace was assembled and knew I had to be in the 1600 BC era. I was a bit of a history buff back in college. Once I made it to the door I stood there as a nice younger women came over to me. She smelled of roses and honey, a smell I did not mind being around. She took me over to the queen. At first glance I could see why he picked her. She was stunning, almost perfect, looking down I noticed her baby bump.

The urge to cry was so hard to fight back. Feeling my now flat tummy remember how I second guessed it all before the accident. But now wishing I just had that one chance to be her mom. The queen snapped me out of my gaze. Turning to the other women she spoke to her saying. Yes, she will do nicely as if I wasn't right there in the room with them.

The queen demanded she get me better clothes and a head dress. She will be my right hand. She has childbearing hips and a strong back bone I can tell in her face. The queen spoke on and on and I just stood while servants undressed me and put me into nicer clothes. Awkward cannot express it. It happened so quickly, servants moving with such haste and grace. Like a musical I get to be a part of. After my transformation I fell into a deep sleep on the nice rug on the queen's floor.

Waking up now expecting this to all be a bad dream, now thinking I have no idea what I'll be doing or how to do it. Hitting the realization I do need Anubis.... I am lost but I'm not asking for help ever. I will never call him. I will not say his name. This will simply have to play out. The morning sun hit my face as the servants got me and the queen ready for another day.

As the queen smiled pleased with her servants, she dismissed them to do the work she had planned out for them. Each one has different tasks from cleaning, to cooking to brainstorming ideas for the following days ahead. She spoke kindly to me now.

Queen: My dear, from now on you are to sleep with me, While I rest you must keep your hand directly on my belly and protect my baby.

This made so much more sense putting this together right-hand childbearing hips she means Dula. Finally, some clarity and some peace, something I could be good at. She walked over to me and put my hands on her belly. She said when you are here and holding my baby you think only happy thoughts.

I told her yes because I do understand just how much a life can mean. Destiney meant everything to me for the last nine months of in my belly I would always hum. This I could tell gave her peace. This would not be so bad if this is all I had to do. Rub a bump and

no negative and unhappy thoughts. My bump is gone but so is my Baby....

7

Love is not enough

The days became shorter, the nights grew longer. The queen and I became closer forming a bond I never knew I could have like a mother I never really had. We laughed all night and talked fondly of the baby all through the day. The love for this baby is what made our bond strong unbreakable.

As I held her bump it was like I could feel the heartbeat of the baby making me feel like I was in the right place at the right time. I could do good here. The queen's gaze became distant. She said she wanted to speak to me about something profoundly serious.

Queen: I have grown so close to you. I only wish you would live out your life here with me. I can offer you a future, I can offer happiness.

For a moment I caught myself wanting to tell her I will always be here. But in my heart knowing this is temporary keeps me from saying these words aloud. As we went to bed, she laid down placing my hands on her belly like always she whispered something so soft to me.

Queen: Rosealine I want you to promise me something.

I looked up at her face, her expression was distant, I could see fear in her eyes for the first time.

Queen: I need you to know the king expects an heir, specifically a boy for this throne. Now I plan to give him this wish, but if I have a girl, please take her run as fast as you can far from here, even away from me. No mother can see her baby killed before her eyes. So, promise me.

As I lay there feeling the pain in her voice I agreed and told her I will do as I 'am asked. She changed her tone and began speaking to the future.

Queen: I know we both know that he is a boy though we can feel it. Would you like to know his name?

Rosealine: Yes of course, I want to know his name he will be the king one day.

Queen: His name will be Anubis.

The words leaving her lips pierced me like a knife in my heart. What did you just say?

Queen: Anubis so noble so strong this is my son.

My mind began to race why he would send me back in time to his birth. Is he really this sick? You have put me in a position of power one move, and I could change the lives of me and other souls. Why would you do this? What is the catch? Now the de-

cisions raced in my mind. But seeing her smile made my mind calm and my body at ease.

He must have known I would fall in love with her. With his mother. She was truly innocent and pure. She was like me not seeing the bad. How could you do this to me Anubis?

That night I got no sleep it was the longest night of my life. Me realizing as I held her, I was also holding you. The power to change lives truly was in my hands. Morning came too soon, but it was like any other day in my now double life. Your face kept appearing in my mind could I really end your life hurt your mother.... Could I see doing to her what you have done to me?

Any day now your mother would give birth to you not knowing who you would become. The creature who has taken everything from me. The what ifs played like a movie in my head she could fall it could be an accident......But these thoughts actually sickened me. Your father would not be forgiving. He would kill her and me too. Ramesses was not a forgiving king.

Days passed that felt like years. Still undecided on what I would do. Would I kill you and take from her what I have lost. Could I really do that to someone else....

You had me right where you wanted me Anubis. The name that now haunts me in the daytime and the night. Day eight and the sun was setting during the time I had spent here. Once more we got ready for bed and as she went to lay down her water broke, and her stomach contracted. She was in labor, tears of joy screams of fear. This was happening whether she or I was ready for it.

Now I was rushing setting up the birthing place getting her comfortable and for a split moment not thinking of you.

Nefertiti! Ramesses called louder and louder.

Ramesses walked into the room as me and the others ran around preparing for your birth. Ramesses stood in the corner as if reminding her to honor him with a boy. His presence was overwhelming. The pressure his gaze made I could even feel. She screamed and she began to push. I had to make up my mind now.

As you were crowning Ramesses walked out without so much as a word not even a smile. That is when I saw the same expression you give cold and restricted.

Icy water and sleepless hours later, she felt exhausted even in birth you were a pain in the ass. Now was my time I walked over to see you I could kill you. This was my choice to kill you now or to become yours later......The taste of the choices in my mouth tasted of despair and bitterness. I picked you up to bring you to her.

She pulled me down to her and whispered you are my blessing. She would never have been able to do this without me. She then looked into your eyes and rubbed your face and spoke.

Neferatiti: Anubis my son my light my morning star. This is your protector.

Was she meaning me.... His what... Right then I knew I could never hurt you or her. Not like this, not now. You had a pure untouched heart your soul was pure you were born new.

I took you over to the bowl of water and cleaned you off for her. Then I walked you to her and handed you over knowing this was over I had lost. I told myself if it were not, you being born it would have had to be someone else fate is fate. I am only glad I had my mind clear Fate can be cruel and usually ends the same no matter the steps before. Clearing my mind, I spoke calmly.

Rosealine: Ok Anubis you win bring me back and face me. I know you are watching me.

Now I became irritated. You truly know how to make me angry. Just like that I was back in the tomb cold dark wet tomb.

Anubis: Rosealine what have I told you about your tone. You will not yell or tell me what to do. Especially since you are at my mercy. Now that you can see you need me and that I do not need you. I want you to beg.

Rosealine: Never, I could never beg you. Never beg to be yours when that's not what I want. No one said I needed you I handled myself just fine.

He snarled a very deep throaty laugh.

Anubis: Are you serious? Do you honestly think I would have sent you to do a real job You could not even kill me. Especially when you have not yet given yourself over to me...I sent you to the one place I knew you would fail. If you choose to defy me again, I will just have to go back on our agreement. After all, what does a mortal really mean to me or you at this point.

Ex, I knew he was talking about you. I can't lose you Destiney needs you; my heart needs to know you are alive. You keep my heart beating even now.

Roselaine: Fine I will be yours

Anubis: Not good enough beg like I said before beg me to take you.

I felt sick but I would do anything for you and Destiney. Even give up my life for you. Let my soul go to save yours. I would give everything for you both to live and have a life.

8

I do not beg?

Rosealine: …. sobs…. Please take me Anubis

Anubis: Wow how pathetic!

Rosealine: I cannot do this; how can you go back on your word do gods not have a code of ethics they follow.

Anubis: My words are as good as yours Rosealine. If you do not keep yours, why would I keep mine?

Rosealine: Please Anubis just let me do your bidding your dirty work. But let me be free to love who I love.

Anubis: I thought you said you do not beg but that is all I hear in your voice now. You are pathetic holding onto a mortal who can never be with you again. I will not change my mind on this Rosealine. I want what I want and if I cannot have it no one will. You will not change my mind, Rosealine. I was being nice and gentle, but I am not above taking what is rightfully mine.

Rosealine: You would not dare touch me Anubis!

Anubis: Let me put this in a way you will understand Rosealine. I am willing to do whatever it takes to make you mine. If that means taking my anger out on the ones you love, then that will be the choice you make.

Rosealine: Is that a threat Anubis....

Anubis: No, I never make threats, I make promises and unlike you I keep my promises.

Now I was the one losing control, all the anger inside me is pouring out. So, I did the most irrational thing in my head I walked overlooked him up and down and punched him right in the face. He did not even flinch. So over and over and over I punched him face, torso, biceps yet nothing not even a sound.

My hand ached increasingly with every blow; my knuckles began to swell but I could not stop myself, nothing was hurting him. After I grew tired and had to stop all I could see was a dark smile on his face. What felt like hours was only minutes. But my anger did not stop there, my fist hurt but my mouth was well rested.

Rosealine: So now I am a joke to you Anubis! I am trying to hurt you and all you can do is smile!

He was nothing like Ex. When we would fight, he would pull me close to him, hug me and restrain me. He never once laid his hands on me never even called me out of my name. His love for me was so pure, so honest. I always said id find a guy like Ex and never let him go...... Funny how life ends up.

Anubis was not Exavier which left me wondering what I am really to Anubis. ... What does he really want from me.... He could have anyone, even someone who might even love him back. Why did he have to choose me?

As this danced around in my head, I found myself blurting it all out before I could catch myself.

Rosealine: You hardly know me why do you want me? I'm of no benefit to you. I have nothing to give you. You could have someone who would really want you.

Now I knew I struck a chord inside him his expression turned ice cold.

Rosealine: Answer me Anubis!

Anubis: I know you Rosealine you may not remember me but I know you! You are as beautiful and hardheaded as all the centuries before. See you see it as if I took you from your life when you are my life. Fate always brings us back together.

Now I was even more confused, he must have lost his mind. He must think I 'am someone else. I went to speak but he turned and walked away into the tomb. Now all that surrounded me was silence. How it this possible how could he know me, and I not know him. He says I have been around for centuries what does that even mean......

I know Egyptians believe in the afterlife. But does that mean recreation too.... I will not over think this he is trying to get into my head to confuse me.

Rosealine: Anubis! You will not win I will not give into you!

For as long as I can remember it had just been me and Exavier. He got me though the ups and downs made me feel I could make it through this world as long as I had him. Have you ever had someone You just know is yours you feel it deep inside your gut. Exavier was always that for me my rock my other half.

That is how I know in my heart he will always be there for Destiney because she came from us, our love. Hours passed......Sitting in silence sulking was getting me nowhere. I did not want to believe him, all I wanted was to feel Ex holding me in his arms kissing my forehead softly. While I held Destiney and kissed her cheek. Hear her soft little coos while I whisper my baby is perfect.

Anubis finally returned, standing now in front of me. But for some odd reason though he felt different, no arrogance or anger that usually surrounds him. He handed me a clay slab.

Rosealine: What is this Anubis I am not going to fall for this.

Anubis: Please Rosealine just take a look at it. What do you have to lose?

Rosealine: Fine only because I know you have the wrong girl.

Picture after picture I saw the story unfolding but I still did not get it. Anubis began to tell the story to illustrate the drawings of the slab.
Anubis: The story goes like this.
His voice has grown on me when he is calm it's nice to hear him speak. This story sounded like a teen novel. The pictures are

so detailed. It is amazing something so old can still be in such great shape. The difference in the pictures is this man and women looked allot more creature like.

The man had a dog face the women a cat both with human robes and head dresses. The bodies were human like though standing on two legs. But back to Anubis telling the story.

Anubis: The story goes like this. The dog faced man fell madly in love with the cat faced women. He would wait for her every night by the tomb just hoping to see her once more. Although it was known they were not made to be. not made for each other the connection they felt was strong. He loved her and she loved him, they saw things in each other no one else could see.

The story says he was the Keeper for the Dead he was to belong in darkness. She was the Keeper of the living and always be-longed in the light. Her name was Bastet she was to protect the Pharos and to spread love to the Egyptians. She was an angel. His name is Anubis......

Rosealine: Wait this is you... this is about you?

Anubis: Hush Rosealine listen to the story...

For once I did as he asked and listened in silence.

Anubis: Anubis was the keeper of the dead; he would collect the lost or wondering souls he was a demon. Bastet never saw him as darkness she fell in love with him and every night she would go to him. Before they knew it their time together shortened. For king Tutt found out about their treachery.

He wanted Bastet for himself, no one could have what he could not. He became enraged and wanted to punish her for her disobedience. He was known to be a cruel and unforgiving king. In his possession he had a mythical dagger. This was the only thing that could kill a god. He knew that Anubis was untouchable for he was already dead. But Bastet was alive, she was an angel. She was the only one he could punish. She would not be the only one king Tutt hurt but to him she was nothing.

She betrayed him and now she would pay the price. Jealousy won him over and overpowered his judgment. This dagger had been crafted from nickel, cobalt, iron and what he called magic. He called for her one night, and she went to his chambers as she did most nights.

When she entered and there was Anubis, they both looked at one another knowing he had found out about them. She walked over to King Tutt and before she could even speak, he slit her throat with the dagger. Anubis cried out for her sorrow in his eyes rage in his heart. Anubis picked up her limp body, carrying her to the tomb weeping knowing her soul would not come to him.

Centuries later a girl appeared to him and right away he felt it Bastet. How was this possible but she explained she was a Tailor of Time, and that this recreation had been going on for centuries. She explained it all from start to finish. Although he could see he would not have her for long he just wanted her. He accepted that no matter what she would always be his in every form.

Anubis turned to me I saw the longing in his eyes. He thinks I am her. No way is this possible. I' am nothing like her Pure or angelic. No, not even close. He must have the wrong girl. So, I had to tell him.

Rosealine: look Anubis I cannot be her I was born and raised in Alabama Auburn to be exact. I had a mom and a dad with a typical life. No magic. Well until now that is.

Anubis: Rosealine you carry her soul inside you. I can feel her inside you.

This was hard to understand that there is more than just me in here?....

Anubis: To you I know you only see that you are just Rosealine but to me I see her in your smile in your eyes I feel her in your touch. That anger in your stomach.

He pulled out the magic dagger the one from the story...

Rosealine: Why do you have that Anubis?

Anubis: So that you would continue to find me repeatedly in life, centuries apart or not. Whenever the dagger is you go. It's fated this dagger has your blood on it so where it lies you go. It pulls you in every time. I know you think I'm crazy Rosealine but I know you can feel it. Stop trying to fight the connection between us. Just let it be, please just let it happen. You might have come back as someone else this time, but you are still Bastet my Bastet.

Rosealine: Anubis please just stop you are not going to get what you want this time. I am not her, she and I are in the same blood line, but we are noting alike. You love someone who is gone.

She is gone Anubis just accept it.

9

Never Ending

*A*nubis: Look! Rosealine How can I make you see you are her. Bastet is inside you whether or not you can see it. I love what you are all forms of you.

Rosealine: Anubis this is crazy you are just lonely and longing for someone who is already gone.

Anubis: Look Rosealine there is a ritual we can do if your heart links to mine you are Bastet. All the memories will come flooding back to you.

Rosealine: Anubis, please let this go let me go.

Anubis: Roselaine we have a lifetime together now the least you can do is humor me. One ritual and if you do not remember I will leave it all alone and I will let you be just my Tailor of Time...

Rosealine: Do you promise me? I have your word as a god as an immortal? If I let you do this, I can have my freedom?

Anubis: I can promise you this Roselaine I will no longer throw myself on you. The only time we will interact is to get *things done professionally in a way of speaking. What I cannot promise you is that I will not still love you or that I won't ever try again forever is a long time. But I promise you will be free to be only a Tailor of Time.*

This was too good to be true id be free to see Ex to see Destiney.

Rosealine: Deal you have my word Anubis.

Anubis: Ok let us begin first let me say you cannot back out or change your mind once started then we must start over. This will be something we have to trust one another to do. Also clear your mind, nothing can be a distraction.

Roselaine: Okay Anubis let us get this over with let me clear my mind.

As it began, I was nervous, all I could hear was his voice chanting words, all I could see was his hands holding up the dagger over his body. I had never really noticed his body before. He was very toned/fit and Beautiful. His dark skin his muscular chest. He was very attractive, I guess I hadn't noticed before. Once the chanting stopped fear set in what was to come next...but I had to keep a clear mind and trust right...

Rosealine: Anubis? Be gentle with me.

He smiled an extremely dangerous smile making my skin crawl with anticipation.

Anubis: Rosealine we must now strip off our clothes we must have our nude bodies exposed.

I was so uncomfortable I did not even want to look at him or have him looking at me. No one had seen me this way except Ex. I had never let anyone see me so exposed vulnerable. I could hear him with every step walking closer to me. I could feel my body tense up. He grabbed my hand placing it against his chest I shivered at the touch. I must have jumped without realizing it.

He told me to relax. His heart was racing but so was mine. He took his other hand and placed it on my chest. I felt a shiver go down my spine. Could I really do this can I go through with this.... I never have let any other man touch me in this way. I whispered I am scared.

Anubis kissed me softly his lips felt like Egyptian cotton so sensual making me forget my fear. I felt power like never before but then Ouch!

Rosealine: What was that?

Before I had even a moment to process, he had stabbed me in the heart with the dagger. How could he betray me this way was this his plan to kill me all along to make my soul forever wonder. To keep my heart in a box locked for eternity.... Was he never actually in love with Bastet. I fell to my knees and the pain was slowly fading. I felt dull, lifeless for the first time through all of this. He rubbed his cold dark hand across my cheek then pulled the dagger out making my lifeless body hit the floor.

He then right before my eyes closed slit his own throat. Was this a Romeo and Juliet suicide......Panic set in and my heart slowed I was really dying this time. But once more my soul hovered over the lifeless body below. I saw Anubis his soul even though I'd never thought he had one was also hovering his creature like body. What is this how are we like this......

I looked at his soul and it was bright shining in a different direction then mine. When I was aware I could feel it or her Bastet. He was right, we are one we are the same. As we returned to our bodies my thoughts came together all I could think is she is who he wants, and I will never be her. He got up and ran to my body saying you have finally come back to me my Bastet. As I woke, I saw the soul of Bastet still hovering over me and in a blink, she entered my body.

Anubis: Now you are one as it should be. Now you are mine forever this time.

I was his now forever...this was never to set me free this was to trap me.

Rosealine: how could you! You tricked me into thinking I would be free but instead you made me and my ancestors one for your own sick pleasure. You made sure she would always be trapped inside me. By placing her blood in me.

Anubis: I am not a god Rosealine like the story said I "am a demon you never stood a chance. I always get what I want.

He grabbed me and kissed me hard, so much aggression so much strength. I was disgusted how was I ever to be free now how could I be so stupid to think he would let me go. His kiss tasted like sin. I was not only his Bastet now but his prisoner. He just kept kissing me. All I could do was cry and all he did was lick my tears and laugh a sinister dark laugh.

He was evil and I never stood a chance. The more he kissed all over my skin the more I felt his lips tainting me. As if pulling all the light from me. A part of me wanted to give in and just be bad. That was the Bastet in me she was my weakness, and he was hers. He knew just how to draw Bastet out of me, and she could take control as the Rosealine took a back seat. He only had to chant, and I no longer had control. That ritual was never to help me remember but to make sure he could have what he wanted.

Anubis: Bastet kiss me now.

The whisper of his voice in my ear was all consuming and before I could react, she/I kissed him. His lips this time tasted sweet and wrong like tart cherries. Forbidden fruit. Then his hands became the problem, every touch was gentle but firm and yet my body played along as if it was also betraying me. I felt like my body was wanting him.

His touch his lips like snake venom he poisoned me. When I tried to fight back it was worse, I bit his lip and made him bleed but that only made him want me more. The fight was over, this was me giving in. He picked me up slamming me into tomb walls my legs wrapped around him his eyes pouring into mine.

Taking control of my thoughts. Bastet wanted this she needed this I could feel her yearning in me. She had truly become my dark side. So, The Rosealine Part of me was sent to the back of my mind. The kisses became sweeter, the movements became magical flawless as if rehearsed for centuries. I could feel him wanting her wanting me. He was pulling my hair and kissing my neck, his body pushing against mine. He grabbed my hand, forcing it down but I did not fight him.

I could feel just how much he needed me. So, I gave in to him. I gave into my dark side (Bastet). As I slid down the wall, I knew exactly what he wanted and exactly how he wanted it.

I looked up into his dark eyes one more time and dropped to my knees. He pushed himself into me. All my stress, anxiety and fear left. I got completely and totally lost in the moment. He tasted of life. As he pulled my head up to his I knew what was to come next. He picked me up again and pushed himself deep into me. The pleasure took over I know he knew because of the sounds escaping my mouth. The sounds from his never sounded so good.

I could feel every inch of him over and over and his tongue like a snake tracing my nipples. I was in a trance. I knew he had me at this moment. I felt it coming and before I could stop everything around me lit up like the northern lights. My legs shook and I knew he felt it too. Destruction. Complete bliss.

Moments later I felt myself regain control. Thinking now with racing thoughts of the horror. The regret. What had I let happen? But as I turned to look at Anubis I felt something for him I never thought id feel. Lust something, I never wanted to feel again. The sad part is someone I fought so hard against I now had feelings for. Hate but also sympathy and even love I know that was the dark side of me, but it was there. Was I growing soft had he worn me down. Or was I always so sinful was this who I really was.... He spoke clearly now. Pulling me out of my own head.

Anubis: Rosealine now that we have become one with each other you should feel my power coursing through your body we can now hear each other's thoughts and feel each other's emotions.

I was silent even though I knew he could now feel the hate rising in me building back up inside me. He said nothing, I could feel his emotions, I knew he felt as if he won. Like I was a trophy he now had in his collection. From this point on I now saw I was his unfortunately he was mine. Looking and thinking back to the clay slab history really has a way of repeating itself.

Sure, king Tutt killed me first, but they were the same man they wanted what they could not have until they got it. From this point on it is a new beginning, a new me no longer Ex and Rosealine and I am sure as hell not Bastet.

From now on I will be Rose the keeper of the living, the tailor of the dead. I will no longer dwell on it, I had work to do and vengeance to plot. One thing I have in me is revenge. I will get you back Anubis one day I will be with Ex and Destiney again. Sometimes you must learn to take fate into your own hands. For now, I'll let you believe you won.

But the long game just started. My job is to help the lost souls and recover the ones they love for a price. For now, Ex had to be history and tomorrow was a new story the beginning of my era to be the Tailor of Time. My mission is to get Anubis on my side let his guard down. One day I will rule the living, and the Dead as Bastet and Anubis will be no more. I am no super-hero, just a girl planning to take back what's mine.

Anubis walked over to me. I knew he could feel the power sourcing through me, but I knew he could flip me like a switch, and I would become what he wanted. I had to learn to control my other side, my darker side. We both knew we had different motives, but we also knew we had a common goal revenge.

The Never Ending ....

www.ingramcontent.com/pod-product-compliance
Lightning Source LLC
Chambersburg PA
CBHW071242130726
47998CB00003B/1024